BOOKMATCH

HOW TO SCAFFOLD STUDENT BOOK SELECTION FOR INDEPENDENT READING

Linda Wedwick & Jessica Ann Wutz

INTERNATIONAL
Reading Association
800 BARKSDALE ROAD, PO BOX 8139
NEWARK, DE 19714-8139, USA
www.reading.org

The International Reading Association attempts, through its publications, to provide a forum for a wide spectrum of opinions on reading. This policy permits divergent viewpoints without implying the endorsement of the Association.

Executive Editor, Books   Corinne M. Mooney
Developmental Editor   Charlene M. Nichols
Developmental Editor   Tori Mello Bachman
Developmental Editor   Stacey Lynn Sharp
Editorial Production Manager   Shannon T. Fortner
Design and Composition Manager   Anette Schuetz

Project Editors   Stacey Lynn Sharp and Rebecca A. Stewart

Cover   Design, Thomson Digital; Photograph, Dianna Dee Damkoehler

The publisher would appreciate notification where errors occur so that they may be corrected in subsequent printings and/or editions.

Library of Congress Cataloging-in-Publication Data

Wedwick, Linda, 1964-
  BOOKMATCH : How to scaffold student book selection for independent
reading / Linda Wedwick, Jessica Ann Wutz.
       p. cm.
  Includes bibliographical references and index.
  ISBN 978-0-87207-619-8
  1. Reading (Elementary)--United States. 2. Children--Books and
reading--United States. 3. Children's literature--Bibliography. I.
Wutz, Jessica Ann, 1974- II. Title.
  LB1573.W393 2008
  372.45'4--dc22

                                                                                              2008013116

This book is dedicated to students like Colby who thrive on choice.

CONTENTS

ABOUT THE AUTHORS

Linda Wedwick is an assistant professor at the Center for Reading and Literacy within the College of Education at Illinois State University, Normal, Illinois, USA. She currently teaches graduate and undergraduate courses in assessment and early adolescent literacy learning. Linda is a former middle school teacher and reading specialist. She has extensively researched self-selection of books and adolescent literature. She is the recipient of the Illinois State University's Clarence W. Sorensen Distinguished Dissertation Award and the Thomas Metcalf Laboratory School's Mary S. Arnold Research Award. She has an authored book chapter in *Shattering the Looking Glass* (2008) edited by Susan S. Lehr in addition to articles that have appeared in *The Reading Teacher*, *Voices From the Middle*, and *Studies in Pop Culture*.

Jessica Ann Wutz is a certified reading specialist and a first-grade teacher at Thomas Metcalf Laboratory School in Normal, Illinois, USA. She is also an instructor of early childhood literacy education at Illinois State University. BOOKMATCH continues to be the focus of her classroom action research. Her articles on BOOKMATCH have appeared in *The Reading Teacher* and *Voices From the Middle*.

Author Information for Correspondence

Linda and Jessica welcome your comments and questions about this book and their research. Please feel free to contact Linda Wedwick at llwedwi@ilstu.edu or contact Jessica Ann Wutz at jawutz@ilstu.edu. You can also visit their website at www.bookmatchforreaders.com.

A recent popular practice in reading instruction has been the movement toward leveling books. The use of book leveling in classroom contexts increased through the use of guided reading (Fountas & Pinnell, 1996), and teachers all over the United States began leveling books in their classroom libraries and steering students toward reading books at a predetermined level. Within guided reading groups, this practice seemed like an excellent strategy for helping young readers learn to read. However, these same leveled books became the focus for all other reading experiences and ultimately limited students' choices. In addition, the leveling of books began making its way into the classrooms of older students. It seemed that teachers thought that if this practice worked for children in first grade it should also work for students in sixth grade.

Teachers of all levels began placing red, green, and orange dots on the books in their classroom libraries and guiding their students toward reading books that were at a level determined by classroom assessment. This raised difficulties. Motivation and interest play a much more critical role in book selection not just for adolescents but also for very young children (Lanier & Lenski, 2008). The trend for leveling books caused a few of us to question whether this popular reading practice should be the extent of a reader's experiences with texts regardless of age.

We began discussing the practice of leveling books in a doctoral class at Illinois State University (ISU) where I was teaching. Linda Wedwick and Jessica Wutz were members of the class. At the time, they were also teachers in local schools. In our discussion, I challenged the class to think about authentic ways that *they* selected books. "How do readers actually select among the thousands of available books?" I asked. "How can teachers in school mimic the natural process of book selection that readers use?"

Linda and Jessica were intrigued. Linda came to the next class with the acronym BOOKMATCH, which described an alternate way for children to select books. The entire class was delighted both with Linda's acronym and with the book-selection process that it described. From that conversation, Jessica decided to conduct teacher research using BOOKMATCH, and an alternative book selection process was created.

BOOKMATCH, as developed by Linda and Jessica, is an easy way to teach students how to select books that they actually *want* to read. BOOKMATCH doesn't disregard the match between a reader's ability and the difficulty of the text. Instead, it creates a questioning process that includes other kinds of criteria as well. It's a process that includes the reader. BOOKMATCH proves to be a practical approach that can be used in reading workshops and in independent reading programs. As a proponent of independent reading, I am excited about the concept of BOOKMATCH and its potential to influence current reading practices. I am delighted that Linda and Jessica took up the challenge of developing a practical approach to book selection that can be easily adapted by readers of all ages.

—Susan Davis Lenski
Professor of Literacy
Portland State University, Portland, Oregon, USA

We feel strongly about allowing students choice in what they read. Other researchers have also found that giving students choice in what they read matters (Atwell, 1998; Bintz, 1993; Chandler-Olcott, 2002; Ivey, 1999; Ivey & Broaddus, 2000; Rog & Burton, 2001/2002). Our beliefs about the importance of independent reading led us to carve out a block of independent reading time in which students would not only read on their own but also choose their own books. Initially, we made an assumption that all readers have intrinsic abilities to choose appropriate books. This misguided assumption led to a reading workshop that lacked appropriate modeling of book-selection strategies. In fact, the concept of "choice" seemed more like a mystery for the students than a strategic attempt at finding a just-right book. We observed students engaged in unproductive activities while choosing books and reading independently. Some students chose books that were too hard, some spent the reading time just browsing books without ever making a selection, and some intermediate readers never finished an entire book in a school year. These reading behaviors led us to reflect on our teaching practices. We realized that successful book selection was not a natural skill for all learners (Chandler-Olcott, 2002). Our conversations resulted in an action research project that investigated ways to support students' choice when self-selecting independent reading materials.

Overview of Initial Study

As teachers and as readers, we brainstormed our own list of criteria when selecting what we wanted to read. We talked to students and other teachers, and we conducted a literature review to explore instruction regarding choice and strategies for book selection. These discussions and the literature review yielded limited information beyond leveling systems. Therefore, we developed a tool to emphasize deliberate strategies for self-selection, which can be used by teachers and students across grade levels as a means of support when choosing books for independent reading time. That tool is BOOKMATCH (Wedwick & Wutz, 2006; Wutz &

Wedwick, 2005), an acronym in which each letter represents a criterion that students can use to select a book for independent reading:

- **B**ook length
- **O**rdinary language
- **O**rganization
- **K**nowledge prior to book
- **M**anageable text
- **A**ppeal to genre
- **T**opic appropriateness
- **C**onnection
- **H**igh-interest

Eighty-six seventh- and eighth-grade students and 22 6-, 7-, and 8-year-olds participated in the initial studies (Wedwick & Wutz, 2006; Wutz & Wedwick, 2005). The focus of the studies was to determine how BOOKMATCH scaffolded students' book selection for independent reading. Data were collected before and after the implementation. Data included whole-group brainstorming, a selection criteria survey, an independent reading attitude survey, reading logs, interviews, and field notes from individual conferences. Results showed that BOOKMATCH presented a snapshot of every student's selection process, produced an independent reading book selection system without the use of levels, promoted awareness of one's self as a literacy learner, and guided instruction for independent reading within a reading workshop.

Through basic literacy experiences like discussing, reading, writing, viewing, listening, and visually representing their understanding of what they read, your students can become aware of themselves as readers. They will continue to increase their reading abilities as well as demonstrate an overall understanding of just-right books in an environment very different from the usual activity-filled elementary classroom. Because of its basic support techniques and frequent reader conferences, and more importantly because of its simplicity, BOOKMATCH will boost the independent reading progress made by students in any grade level, but especially in the elementary grades. We consider BOOKMATCH to be the crux of our reading workshop.

Influences on Our Teaching

Social constructivist theory has guided our instruction as well as our development of BOOKMATCH. We approach teaching from a social constructivist perspective, embracing Vygotsky's (1978) Zone of Proximal Development, which he describes as "the distance between the actual developmental level as determined through problem solving and the level of potential development as determined through problem solving under adult guidance or in collaboration with more capable peers" (p. 84). Simply put, the students in our classrooms can "learn new skills and strategies that they cannot learn on their own" with the help and scaffolding of a teacher or peer (Robb, 2004, p. 5). We believe that students construct their own knowledge by connecting new information to prior knowledge and experience. This process of knowledge construction is further influenced by the social contexts in which the learner encounters new information. The learner's construction of knowledge is affected by interactions with the environment and with peers and adults in that environment.

Another influence on our teaching and on the development of BOOKMATCH was Cambourne's Conditions for Literacy Learning. According to Cambourne (1988), the following conditions must exist in order for students to learn:

- Immersion: creating a print-rich environment in which students are immersed throughout the day

- Demonstration: providing the learners with opportunities to see experts using language and literacy

- Approximation: offering a safe environment in which students learn to become experts and "try out" new concepts

- Expectations: establishing expectations in which learners expect to succeed and feel capable of succeeding

- Employment: allowing learners plenty of opportunities to practice and use strategies or skills both independently and with others

- Responsibility: letting students make their own decisions, including what they learn as well as how they will express their understanding

- Response: the immediacy and amount of feedback students receive both from the teacher as well as their peers as they become expert users of language and literacy

- Engagement: the learner's desire to attend to and actively participate in the learning

Like Cambourne, Routman (2003) shares a way of thinking about conditions that maximize learning. Her Optimal Learning Model Across the Curriculum explains how demonstration and shared demonstration lead to independence in which responsibility is ultimately handed over to the students. According to Routman, "with expert assistance and encouragement, learners gradually move from dependence to independence" (p. 44).

Cambourne and Routman inspired us to identify the pattern of implementing BOOKMATCH and the Phases of Learning that are loosely based on their models of learning (see Figure 1). Over the years, we have

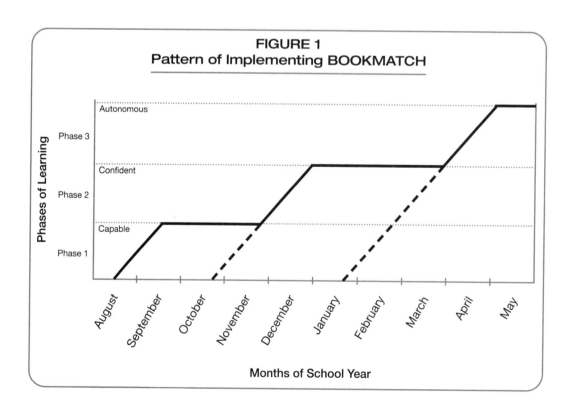

FIGURE 1
Pattern of Implementing BOOKMATCH

Phases of Learning

Phase 3 — Autonomous

Phase 2 — Confident

Capable

Phase 1

Months of School Year

August, September, October, November, December, January, February, March, April, May seen a pattern of implementing BOOKMATCH as students progress through the acts of self-selection and independent reading. This pattern of implementation illustrates the phases literacy learners go through across the school year while the teacher implements BOOKMATCH. These phases are highlighted in Chapters 2 through 4 to show you approximately where your readers should be. However, keep in mind that this pattern should be used as a guideline only—even though this pattern is appropriate for average readers, some teachers may have to adjust the pattern if their students are below or above average. Therefore, use your students as a guide for implementing BOOKMATCH and judge for yourself when they are ready for more responsibility.

Throughout the book, we will use the terms *capable*, *confident*, and *autonomous* to describe our learners as they go through the Phases of Learning to develop the self-selection strategies acquired through BOOKMATCH. Phase 1: Capable introduces students to BOOKMATCH and takes readers through the initial establishment of routines within independent reading time. Phase 2: Confident is dominated by practice as students take on more responsibility for their own learning. Finally, Phase 3: Autonomous continues to build on what was learned in the first two phases; however, the reader's successful self-selection becomes more habitual. We believe that all students begin as capable learners who deserve numerous opportunities for success. This success leads learners to a more confident state of mind. The learner's belief that he or she is capable lays the foundation for the learner to be autonomous. Moving through these phases, readers will experience periods of learning plateaus and peaks. At times, the readers seem to hold constant, until your instruction creates additional opportunities for upward movement. We will refer to our pattern of implementing BOOKMATCH throughout this book and in the chapters describe in more detail the self-selection behaviors exhibited by students as they move through these phases of instruction.

How This Book Is Structured

We've organized this book like a typical school year, emphasizing the Phases of Learning during implementation. As the chapters unfold, keep in mind that many activities described happen simultaneously rather than sequentially or step-by-step. Therefore, you will find that all of the chapters are intertwined. Together, the chapters provide a guide for setting up and managing an effective independent reading time in which students fully engage in the practice of reading while building a positive attitude. Chapter 1, "Introduction: Understanding BOOKMATCH and the Reading Workshop Approach," creates a context for using BOOKMATCH within a reading workshop. In Chapter 2, "Getting Started: Sorting and Setting Up for a BOOKMATCH Classroom," teachers are presented with practical suggestions for setting up their classrooms and preparing for their capable readers. We recommend that you read Chapters 1 and 2 before reading the other chapters and before you implement BOOKMATCH because these two chapters lay a foundation for understanding critical terms and concepts. Chapter 3, "Implementing BOOKMATCH: Moving Capable Readers to Confidence," shows how teachers model their reading process through thinking aloud and conversing with their students. The chapter provides guidelines for the teacher's role and teacher scripts for independent reading time and when using BOOKMATCH. Chapter 4, "Moving Toward Independence: Confident Learners Become Autonomous," offers examples of confident and autonomous learners empowered by shared demonstration. Student work samples and transcripts of student sharing are included. Chapter 5, "Managing the Data: Accountability and Conferences With BOOKMATCH," explains the aspects of assessment and record keeping in an independent reading program, emphasizing the importance of reading conferences for making instructional decisions. Finally, Chapter 6, "Measures of Success: Portraits of BOOKMATCH Readers," defines a continuum of reading behaviors and details three readers' experiences with BOOKMATCH. All names used throughout the book are pseudonyms for actual students. Additionally, an appendix includes reproducible copies of forms and surveys discussed throughout the book.

Special features included within the chapters are Clarification Spots, Tips for Intermediate-Grade Readers, Parent Connections, and Reflection Points. The Clarification Spots provide *our* definitions of commonly used terms and helpful tips for your instruction. Tips for Intermediate-Grade Readers suggest adaptations for teaching older or more advanced literacy learners. Parent Connections offer ideas for ongoing communication and reinforcement at home. Each chapter concludes with a Reflection Point that will help you consider your own practices and beliefs and get the most from this text.

Who Should Read This Book?

Although many of our examples and discussions in this book took place in a first-grade classroom, BOOKMATCH has been used successfully in all elementary grades. Teachers of intermediate-level students will find Tips for Intermediate-Grade Readers embedded within the chapters, as well as a modified BOOKMATCH form (see Table 2 in Chapter 1). Regardless of the grade level you teach, this book provides the fundamental principles needed to implement BOOKMATCH. The intended audiences include all elementary teachers, preservice teachers, librarians, and administrators. This book would be an excellent choice for a teacher study group. It is our hope that teachers find the book to be practical yet supported by research and theory as well as their own observations. BOOKMATCH has the potential to affect a large number of readers in today's classrooms who deserve opportunities for unrestricted self-selection.

Acknowledgments

Linda would like to thank her husband, Steve, and her son for their love and encouragement.

Jessica would like to thank her family and particularly her husband, John, for his love and patience.

Together we appreciate our colleagues who supported us in the process of writing this book, especially those who used BOOKMATCH in their own classrooms. Thank you to Kerrie Glintborg-Reed, who went out of her way to provide ongoing encouragement. She kept us motivated to continue writing and reminded us of the importance of sharing our work. Susan Davis Lenski was there when BOOKMATCH was just an idea, and we thank her for pushing us to research this idea and disseminate its success. Thank you to Dianna Dee Damkoehler, who supplied an endless number of books to our classrooms and was always eager to take photographs. All classroom photographs in the book were taken by Dee.

Finally, we want to thank the International Reading Association for having faith in BOOKMATCH and suggesting that we pursue writing this book.

CHAPTER 1

Introduction: Understanding BOOKMATCH and the Reading Workshop Approach

"It is the teacher's role to help students develop strategies for selecting appropriate books—books that involve their interests and support their ability as readers."

—Cora Lee Five & Kathy Egawa, "Reading and Writing Workshop: What Is It and What Does It Look Like?" in *School Talk*

In today's classrooms, it is essential to create a structure that emphasizes independent reading. In general, independent reading programs for elementary classrooms will contain similar components. However, the success of independent reading is greatly dependent upon *what* students are reading. Independent reading time is most effective when students are reading appropriate, just-right books for their individual skill levels as well as personal preference—something not often provided through leveled, teacher-selected books. In fact, students can best find their just-right books when they are given the power of choice and are able to self-select the books they read during independent reading time. However, not all readers have intrinsic abilities to choose appropriate books; many students must be taught how to develop strategies for selecting appropriate books.

By using a tool called BOOKMATCH during the independent reading time of a reading workshop, students can learn to strategically select appropriate just-right books. In this chapter we define BOOKMATCH, its role in reading workshop, and the importance of independent reading. Because we view independent reading as a critical component for using BOOKMATCH, we share our own understanding of this period of time within a reading workshop. Finally, we present the many benefits of using BOOKMATCH with your readers.

What Is BOOKMATCH?

BOOKMATCH is an instructional tool that enables students to engage in the free, voluntary reading of just-right, self-selected reading material. BOOKMATCH helps readers choose books that are just right for them. Each letter of BOOKMATCH is a criterion for selection, as illustrated in Table 1 (a reproducible poster version of the BOOKMATCH criteria can be found in the Appendix). Inherent in BOOKMATCH is the understanding that no two readers are the same and that when matching students to books for independent reading time, different criteria for each individual reader need to be taken into consideration. Neither you nor your students will need to worry or think about the levels of the books in terms of numbers. After all, think of yourself as a reader. The last thing you want is

TABLE 1
BOOKMATCH

Letter	Criteria
B	Book Length
O	Ordinary Language
O	Organization
K	Knowledge Prior to Book
M	Manageable Text
A	Appeal to Genre
T	Topic Appropriateness
C	Connection
H	High-Interest

to be limited to the books found in basket 7 or to books with the pink dots. Using BOOKMATCH, your students will simply search for just-right books.

BOOKMATCH involves a process of asking questions, interacting with a text, and making decisions about a book. This tool allows readers to emphasize their personal preferences. Elementary students may not yet realize their preferences as readers. Therefore, we want them to think about each criterion when making book selections until this process becomes automatic. Some students will realize that certain criteria matter more than others when they find a just-right book. For students to find success with BOOKMATCH, they should understand these criteria and take the time to think about the book in hand and themselves as readers.

The BOOKMATCH terminology is appropriate for all grade levels (including those beyond the elementary grades). However, in order to simplify the use with primary-grade readers, you may choose to use the sample criteria and supporting questions designed for 6-, 7-, and 8-year-olds (see Table 2 and pages 111–112). Readers in the intermediate grades and perhaps some of your more advanced primary-grade readers may be ready for more sophisticated questions regarding book selection. Therefore, Table 2 also provides an alternative designed for 9- to 12-year-olds. Each version of BOOKMATCH is slightly different, with the goal of providing developmental and differential support for readers. You can decide which version will work best for your students based on their prior knowledge and current self-selection skills.

Each selection criterion found within BOOKMATCH has clear purposes behind the questions, regardless of grade level. Table 3 will help you see and better understand the purpose of each criterion and how these purposes align with the supporting book-selection questions that correspond with each criterion. Please use this chart as your guide when working with independent readers one on one. We've found it helpful to have this on a clipboard or within a conference notebook as a guide to refer to with the reader. It will remind you of the basics, while breaking down each part of the acronym. As you confer with students, we encourage you to share the Purpose section with the students, as well, so they know in what ways you are helping them as readers. The remaining sections in this chapter explain how BOOKMATCH can fit into your reading workshop approach.

TABLE 2
BOOKMATCH Criteria and Supporting Questions
Modified According to Grade Level

A. BOOKMATCH for Primary-Grade Readers

Criteria	Questions and Statements to Support This Criterion
Book Length	• Is this length too little, just right, or too much?
Ordinary Language	• Does it make sense and sound like talk?
Organization	• How is the book structured?
Knowledge Prior to Book	• What do I already know about this topic, this book, or this author?
Manageable Text	• Are the words too easy, just right, or too hard?
Appeal to Genre	• What is the genre and do I know this genre?
Topic Appropriateness	• Am I comfortable with the topic of this book?
Connection	• Can I relate and make a connection to another book or real life experience?
High-Interest	• Am I interested in finding out more?

B. BOOKMATCH Criteria for Intermediate-Grade Readers

Criteria	Questions and Statements to Support This Criterion
Book Length	• Is this a good length for me? • Do I feel like committing to this book?
Ordinary Language	• Turn to any page and read aloud. • Does the text sound natural? • Does it flow? Does it make sense?
Organization	• How is the book structured? • Are chapters short or long?
Knowledge Prior to Book	• Read the title, view the cover page, or read the summary on the back of the book. • What do I already know about this topic, this book, or this author?
Manageable Text	• Begin reading the book. • Will this book provide the right amount of challenge? • Do I understand what I read?
Appeal to Genre	• What is the genre? • Have I read this genre before? • What can I expect from this genre?
Topic Appropriateness	• Am I comfortable with the topic of this book? • Do I feel like I am ready to read about this topic?
Connection	• Can I relate to this book? • Can I make a connection?
High-Interest	• Am I interested in this book? • Do others recommend this book? • What is my purpose for reading this book?

TABLE 3
Breaking Down BOOKMATCH

Criteria	Questions and Statements to Support This Criterion	Purpose
B Book Length	• Is this a good length for me? • How long is this book compared to what I am used to reading? • Is it too little, just right, or too much? • Do I feel like committing to the length of this book?	The reader needs to think about whether he or she is comfortable with the length of the book, but it should provide the right amount of challenge. Is he or she aware of the number of pages before he or she starts reading?
O Ordinary Language	• Turn to any page and read aloud. • Does the text flow? • Does it make sense? • Does it sound like talk? • Is it written in a way that I can understand it?	The reader is testing the style of writing and whether or not he or she is comfortable with reading the book written in this way. Readers need to be aware of how style of writing impacts how it is read. For example, an I Spy book is merely a list of words separated by commas. This style does not allow a reader to practice reading strategies and should not be read for language sense. Also, poetry often does not sound like talk unless the reader knows something about meter, rhythm, and rhyme.
O Organization	• How is the book structured? • Are there text and illustrations? Are there chapters, charts, talking bubbles, headings, or captions? • Am I comfortable with the print size and number of words on a page? • Are chapters short or long? • Is there a table of contents, summary, and glossary? • Are there words in bold or italics?	The reader is looking at the book as a whole and realizing the ways the author can choose to share information. The structure of the book can help support a reader's understanding when he or she knows the reason for the way the book is organized. The reader can use the structure of the book to support comprehension.
K Knowledge Prior to Book	• Read the title, view the cover page, or read the summary on the back of the book. • What do I already know about this topic, this book, this author, or this illustrator? • Have I heard this book read aloud or seen the movie?	The reader is asked to think about his or her current knowledge of the topic, book in general, and author. This activates the reader's schema and builds on his or her knowledge.

(continued)

TABLE 3 (continued)
Breaking Down BOOKMATCH

Criteria	Questions and Statements to Support This Criterion	Purpose
M Manageable Text	• Begin reading the book. • Are the words in the book easy, just right, or hard? • Do I understand what I read? • Am I able to use the five-finger rule successfully? • Will this book provide the right amount of challenge?	Readers give the book a try with the focus being the difficulty of the text. Readers need to have an understanding of metacognition or being able to track the amount of difficult words. Most important, readers need to be able to have an understanding of the passage they just read.
A Appeal to Genre	• What is the genre? • Have I read this genre before? • Do I know about this genre? • What can I expect from this genre?	Readers need to think back to their previous reading experiences with class read-alouds and independent reading. They then think through what they know about this type of genre, setting expectations for story elements. For example, if the reader has read a mystery before, he or she can activate the schema for a mystery.
T Topic Appropriateness	• What is the topic of this book? • Am I comfortable with the topic of this book? • Do I feel like I am ready to read about this topic?	Readers make a decision here with the focus being the topic of the book. Literature can share information with readers about many topics, some serious or mature in nature. It is important for the reader to be prepared for such topics. Some examples across the grade levels include death and dying, homelessness and poverty, racism, relationships, and war.
C Connection	• Can I relate to this book? • Does this book remind me of anything or anyone? • Can I make a connection to another book or real life experience?	The reader takes some time to think about his or her own experiences up to this point and how they may relate, even in a small way, to the book in hand. This connection will support engagement. Connection may be to self, another text, or to the world.
H High-Interest	• Am I interested in this book? • Am I interested in finding out more? • Do others recommend this book? • What is my purpose for reading this book?	The reader will now rate his or her own interest in the book chosen. The reader is deciding whether he or she has high interest. Anything less may not support engagement through the entire text.

The Role of BOOKMATCH in Reading Workshop

BOOKMATCH is a perfect fit for the reading workshop approach to literacy instruction used in many elementary classrooms today. In fact, BOOKMATCH can become one of the most important components of reading workshop, because this approach provides opportunities for you to model reading for students and then opportunities for students to share their readings with you. According to the literature (Calkins, 2001; Hindley, 1996; Routman, 2003), a reading workshop is a designated, uninterrupted time each day that allows for the following basic literacy components: read-alouds, minilessons, modeling, guided groups, conferences, ongoing assessments, and independent reading. While BOOKMATCH is a tool that is specifically used during the independent reading block of reading workshop, each of these components of reading workshop can be used with BOOKMATCH. A BOOKMATCH classroom using the reading workshop approach may use these literacy components in the following ways:

- **Read-alouds** are typically used in reading workshop as a springboard and as a source of information for a variety of **minilessons** on words, topics, themes, author studies, and more. With BOOKMATCH, read-alouds are the examples used in minilessons to show the types of books that readers will be selecting from and their characteristics.

- **Modeling** is an opportunity for the teacher to show by doing. The teacher goes beyond telling students what to do by actually doing the task himself or herself in front of the group. With BOOKMATCH, modeling is used daily to explain each criterion but also to demonstrate techniques for self-selection. For example, when teaching browsing you can explain to students that it is a way to scan a text, by looking at a few of the pages and thinking about what they're seeing. At the same time you can hold a book and turn the pages to demonstrate browsing.

- A **guided group** is a temporary small group of readers who come together for a particular purpose. This teacher-led experience provides explicit instruction based on the needs of the readers. A guided group with BOOKMATCH may include a group of readers who need help with understanding the different ways that books are structured and organized.

- **Conferences** provide an opportunity for the teacher to learn more about each reader in the classroom, as this is one-on-one time with a specific purpose. A typical reading workshop conference allows time for the teacher to sit with a reader and confer about his or her book, how it's going, and if any clarification or support is needed. These same conferences happen when using BOOKMATCH, only the conference discussions will include questioning the hows and whys of choosing the book. Notes taken during these conferences provide ongoing assessment.

- **Independent reading** is a designated amount of time when students read on their own, without teacher support. We feel strongly about including this daily reading time within a workshop and make it a point to have students use BOOKMATCH as their support to self-select just-right books.

Reading workshop requires large blocks of time in order to include a minilesson, modeling by the teacher, and then for students to go off on their own to practice what they've learned while being engaged in reading materials. Table 4 offers various options for allocating the components of reading workshop within an elementary classroom. The time frames are flexible, but your daily routine should be consistent because each component is as important as the next. The structured format of the reading workshop and its components creates a learning environment in which the teacher can work one-on-one with students, and students can work on individual goals, read what interests them, and expand their understanding of various topics. It's the ideal situation—it's differentiated instruction.

TABLE 4
Daily Reading Workshop Options for the Elementary Grades

Whole-Group Instructional Options (10–25 min.)	• Read-aloud • Minilesson on specific skill, reading strategy, BOOKMATCH, author, or genre related to read-aloud • Independent practice of minilesson • Word study and vocabulary • Fluency practice • Phonemic awareness
Independent Reading Learner Options (30–45 min.)	• Independent reading • Guided groups • Conferences • Browsing books • Self-selection
Wrap-Up Options (5–15 min.)	• Reading Log • Sharing time • Clean up

Differentiated instruction describes the approach a teacher takes to meet the needs of each student as a unique learner. Because students come to a reading event with varying interests and knowledge, you will need to adjust your instruction based on each student's Zone of Proximal Development (ZPD; Vygotsky, 1978). The ZPD is the place at which a learner needs support in order to make progress. Eventually, this support allows the learner to perform the task independently. According to Tomlinson (1999), "teachers must be ready to engage students in instruction through different learning modalities, by appealing to differing interests, and by using varied rates of instruction along with varied degrees of complexity" (p. 2). In differentiated instruction, the instruction accommodates the student rather than changing overall curriculum goals. In a reading workshop and with BOOKMATCH, if your goal for a specific learner is to practice reading fluently, that learner could accomplish this goal regardless of her interests or ability as long as she is reading a self-selected, just-right book.

Teachers and researchers agree that it's better to differentiate instruction (e.g., Grosvenor, 2004; Tomlinson, 1999); however, "the

Depending on their daily schedule, advanced readers in the upper elementary grades may not have 45–60 minute blocks of time for independent reading. Therefore, to increase time spent reading, we recommend at least 10 minutes each day during school in conjunction with expectations for at-home reading.

challenge lies in translating that belief into action" (Willis & Mann, 2000, ¶ 7). We have found that using a reading workshop focused on independent reading—and the self-selection of materials by students for that independent reading through BOOKMATCH—takes away the challenge of differentiating. The real challenge would be trying to find one book that meets the needs of all 25 readers in a classroom. The very nature of BOOKMATCH within the reading workshop approach presented in this chapter is differentiated because students are consistently working with self-selected texts that are within their ZPD. Differentiation takes place through the use of small groups, conferences, and student choice.

Tomlinson (1999) describes three ways to differentiate: content, process, and products. Content differentiation refers both to the concepts and the means of teaching those concepts. For example, during reading workshop, a teacher may focus on the skill of "chunking" words (covering parts of a word). Dry-erase boards and new vocabulary may be used with one group of students, while another group may use familiar words and an actual text to learn the concept of chunking. Process differentiation is related to the kinds of activities that learners engage in to practice or apply the concepts taught. One group may echo the teacher's modeling of chunking a word, and another group may follow step-by-step directions. Products differentiation refers to the variety of ways in which you allow students to express their understanding of the concepts (Willis & Mann, 2000). Students may turn to a neighbor and demonstrate how to chunk an unknown word or they may tell another reader the directions for chunking, or they can use a sticky note to mark pages in their self-selected book where they have used the chunking strategy.

Within a reading workshop that implements BOOKMATCH, content differentiation includes teaching how to self-select by using many different criteria like genre, book length, the text, the topic, the nature of connections to the text, background knowledge, the structure of the text, and what it means to be interested. Process differentiation includes such tasks as sorting books, participating in book talks, turning and talking to partners, browsing the books, interviewing readers, and conferring with a teacher. Product differentiation may take place through presenting book talks, using a share chair, participating in small groups, maintaining reading logs, filling out student comment forms, and writing on sticky notes placed throughout the text. These ways of differentiating are shared in more detail in later chapters.

Defining Independent Reading and Understanding the Importance of Self-Selection

While Krashen (2001) calls independent reading free voluntary reading, you might refer to independent reading as Sustained Silent Reading (SSR) or Drop Everything And Read (DEAR). Pilgreen (2000) outlines eight factors for successful SSR programs: accessibility to texts, books that are appealing, a conducive environment, encouragement, staff training, nonaccountability, follow-up activities, and time to read. Whatever you call it, each student deserves independent reading time separate from the daily teacher-directed instruction that takes place during whole-group minilessons and guided groups. Independent reading is an opportunity for your students to experience success with reading in a school context. Whether a student is a strong or emerging reader, daily responsibility and control of their learning as an independent reader ensures some level of success.

As classroom teachers, we continually observe and document evidence that suggests independent reading not only supports students' reading growth, but also promotes positive attitudes toward reading when student choice is involved. Yoon's (2002) study found "affirmative evidence for significant reading attitude gains from a fixed period of time for students [that] read materials of their own choosing either for pleasure or for information" (p. 186). While the *Report of the National Reading Panel* (National Institute of Child Health and Human Development, 2000) claims that there are not enough well-designed studies to confirm a causal link between reading achievement and independent reading, *Becoming a Nation of Readers* (Anderson, Hiebert, Scott, & Wilkinson, 1985) alternately suggests that priority should be given to independent reading in the classroom. As Krashen (2001) and others argue, free voluntary reading in school is essential for reading growth:

> It is only by omitting a large number of relevant studies—and misinterpreting the ones that were included—that the NRP was able to reach the startling conclusion that there is no clear evidence that encouraging children to read more actually improves reading achievement. (p. 119)

Therefore, our definition of independent reading involves more than simply having students read silently on their own. Although influenced by the writing of many (e.g., Calkins, 2001; Cambourne, 1988; Goodman, 1985; Rosenblatt, 1991; Routman, 2003), *our* definition of independent reading is as a significant component of a reading curriculum in which students engage in voluntary reading of just-right, self-selected reading material. Therefore, the main purpose for independent reading time within reading workshop is to allow students to self-select just-right books on their own and to spend time engaged in reading those books. We are talking about a time to teach strategies for self-selection and for students to practice strategies for self-selection. It is a time when "readers consolidate the skills and strategies they have been taught and come to own them" (Allington, 2005/2006, p. 16). The overall goal of independent reading time is that the students place themselves with just-right books, and that they not rely on a leveled or teacher-selected book. We don't want a student to spend time browsing a text that is too easy or too difficult, or teachers to choose the books that students read during independent reading.

It is important that your independent reading time be just that—time spent reading: "As habitual readers are well aware, the very knowledge that they have to do something with reading other than what they choose to do takes away from its magic" (Pilgreen, 2000, p. 15). We do not suggest using centers during this time, setting up other work for students to do in order to stay busy and on task, or having students work on literacy activities that have separate purposes. A great way to maintain students' interest in reading is to keep the focus on reading. Pilgreen (2000) suggests that teachers "omit any activity that gives students the message that they are responsible for completing a task, comprehending a particular portion of their reading, or showing they have made improvement in some way" (p. 15). We agree that no activity or specific worksheet needs to be involved during independent reading; however, we want our students to know that comprehension is important and that good readers do continue to improve. This is a meaningful time for the students to be engaged and also to sharpen their reading strategies.

This time is provided with the clear purpose of reading just-right materials and your students need this message communicated to them from the beginning. It's inevitable that a student will come to you and say something like, "What can we do if we don't want to read?" Alysse (all student names are pseudonyms) was one such questioning student. She was reminded, "This is our independent reading time, so you need to be a reader. I can help you with your choice of books. Would you like that?"

There are a few aspects of our definition of independent reading that warrant further discussion. First, independent reading must be a *significant component* of your reading workshop. Any one reading workshop component used alone would not be sufficient for students' reading improvement, yet in classrooms that we've observed, the components seem out of balance. Independent reading is not always viewed as a main component of the reading workshop but rather a luxury if time allows. Often independent reading is only provided as an extra option to students who finish their work sooner than others, which means that those students who are already strong in literacy skills continue to get extra practice. Stanovich (1986) refers to this as the Matthew Effect, whereby the rich get richer and the poor get poorer. We believe that independent reading is an essential daily component of a quality reading workshop that all students deserve.

> **CLARIFICATION SPOT**
>
> *Just-right* can be defined as describing reading material in which the reader has considered several aspects and made decisions about the viability of a match between the reader and the text. Just-right can also be defined as describing a text that supports a student's particular purpose for reading.

A second important aspect of our definition is the emphasis on *just-right, self-selected materials*. We believe that books leveled for difficulty and selected by the teacher can have their place in some reading curricula, but during independent reading time, students must have the opportunity to learn and apply strategies for self-selection based on their own interests, ability, and prior knowledge. Books leveled for difficulty— as made popular by Fountas and Pinnell (1996)—have become the norm with teachers from kindergarten through middle school. Leveled texts can provide a tool for supporting a teacher in matching books to students for a guided reading lesson, but students should not be aware of these levels, nor should they be the extent of students' choices for independent reading. Rog and Burton (2001/2002) explain that students must learn to self-select reading material in order to maintain their interest in reading:

Leveled books are only one type of reading resource available to students. If we restrict all of the students' independent reading choices to our collections of leveled books, we jeopardize the motivation that comes from self-selection of reading materials. Interest and background knowledge will have a significant impact on the readability of a text for a particular student. Therefore, it is important for all students to learn to self-select reading materials that will be interesting and accessible to them. (p. 355)

A review of the literature confirms that others have expressed similar concerns about leveled books (Routman, 2003; Szymusiak & Sibberson, 2001).

Like Pierce (1999) we are concerned about how students define themselves as readers when much of their reading material is based on books leveled for difficulty that a teacher selects for the student to read. Independent reading material should not be constrained by arbitrary numbers, colors, and letters on books that are placed into a student's book box or reading bag. From our perspective, reading material is worthy of the just-right label when a student has thought about various criteria for selection and made decisions about its appropriateness.

Finally, by using *reading materials* in our definition of independent reading, we are suggesting that students should be able to select any reading material that interests them. These reading materials may include books, magazines, or newspapers, as well as other "texts" that you feel are appropriate for your students, including multimedia texts. Throughout these chapters, we use the term *book* as an encompassing word for any reading material that a student may choose.

Benefits of Incorporating BOOKMATCH as Part of Your Classroom Routine

There are numerous benefits of using the BOOKMATCH tool in your classroom as a part of the independent reading block of reading workshop. For one, using BOOKMATCH enables students to increase reading endurance and have time to simply be readers. At the beginning of each school year, 15 minutes of independent reading seems like an eternity. However, with the implementation of BOOKMATCH, longer periods of independent reading become possible. We work up to 45 minutes by midyear and 60 continuous minutes by the end of April. Morrow, Pressley, Smith, and Smith (1997) share the belief that reading achievement can increase with an increase of engaged reading. We agree. BOOKMATCH provides more quality, engaged reading time because the reading material is self-selected. When a reader is armed with the right combination of preferred criteria the rate of abandonment decreases, which increases the engagement between the reader and the text (Rosenblatt, 1991).

In addition, BOOKMATCH enables students to use the independent reading time to practice using self-selection and to apply reading comprehension strategies independently, such as using picture clues, reading to the end of the sentence and going back to reread, and so on. The criteria of BOOKMATCH not only assist students during the selection process, but also provide a scaffold for monitoring during reading. Independent readers will monitor their book choice by asking questions about what they read. Do I continue to be engaged? Do I continue to be committed to the book length? Am I making connections? Their views may change as they interact with more of the text.

Similarly, with BOOKMATCH, students are motivated to read voluntarily. Reading becomes a daily habit. Once they define themselves as readers, rather than question why they are having reading time, they begin to question why they are not. If students miss their reading time, they will want to know why. As confident readers, many of our first graders choose reading during open center time.

As a result of BOOKMATCH, you'll acquire formative data to guide daily instruction. You'll have plenty of opportunities for kidwatching (Goodman, 1985) because students work independently. Kidwatching is a form of assessment through observation that allows teachers to see students' responses to our instruction and the learning environment. During shared demonstration, any confusion or accomplishment is exposed. This data informs your instructional decisions to be used with whole groups, guided groups, and in conferences. Similarly, you'll acquire summative data as evidence of reading progress. You and your students will have documentation of learning that includes running records, reading logs, anecdotal notes, and student comment forms. This data is the evidence of students moving from capable to autonomous learners (see Chapters 2 through 4).

In the real world books are not leveled. Readers must learn the strategies for matching themselves to books rather than relying on their teachers. Successful matches build confidence. When readers read books that interest them, they are more likely to view reading as an avenue for lifelong learning. Only 40% of children between 5–8 years old read every day for fun. Even more alarming is that when children reach 9–11 years old, the percentage drops to 29 and continues to decrease through age 17 ("Keeping Kids Reading," 2006). Perhaps most important, with BOOKMATCH, students develop the effective habits of lifelong literacy learners.

Reflection Point

Take a moment to reflect on and record your own beliefs regarding the value of independent reading. What do you currently do to teach self-selection strategies?

CHAPTER 2

Getting Started: Sorting and Setting Up for a BOOKMATCH Classroom

"Children need at least thirty minutes a day to read books they can read, preferably of their choosing."
—Lucy Calkins, *The Art of Teaching Reading*

Setting up the classroom is a crucial part of the success of BOOKMATCH and the success of your capable readers to choose just-right texts. Your preparation will begin before your students even arrive; however, they need to experience a sense of ownership as well, especially when it comes to the books in the classroom library. In this chapter, we describe how to prepare the classroom for readers and how to prepare readers for BOOKMATCH. Once you prepare the environment of the classroom, it will be important to get to know your students through interviews and surveys as you establish routines together, which will also be described in this chapter. Then, you will learn how to get started with BOOKMATCH as we share the process of immersing your students in the sorting of books and show you how to give your first lessons on BOOKMATCH. The chapter also presents a pattern for implementing BOOKMATCH and discusses the importance of seeing your students as capable readers early on.

Preparing Your Classroom for Readers

As the teacher, your initial role is to create a classroom environment that is comfortable and inviting. Your classroom should include comfortable seating, space for lounging with a book or walking around, a variety of plants, and many nooks and containers in which to store books (see Figure 2). A table should be available for those who choose that as their reading place. And, of course, books!

A "strong classroom library" is essential, as it supports the act of students being "matched with books they can read" and want to read (Routman, 2003, p. 80). Your library needs an ample supply of unleveled literature. Common reading workshop materials include magazines, brochures, newspapers, anthologies, picture books, chapter books, series

FIGURE 2
Comfortable and Inviting Classroom Environment
With Ample Space for Readers

Photograph by Dianna Dee Damkoehler. Used with permission.

books, Big Books, joke and riddle books, informational texts, and students' published work. Your school or local librarian can support you in filling your shelves with print in multiple genres, from fiction to nonfiction and poetry. Obtain multiple copies of some texts you know will be popular. Books should vary in difficulty, structure, length, genre, and topic—all the criteria that BOOKMATCH encourages a student to think about. Just because you teach third grade, for instance, you shouldn't limit your collection to only texts leveled, suggested, or labeled for third graders. This is another chance to provide differentiated instruction, while giving students the feeling that they are capable of taking charge of their own choices. Your available books should be diverse, rich, and inviting as well as informational.

Large clear containers should be used to display and store books (see Figure 3). We found them at local hardware or department stores.

FIGURE 3
Book Containers and Book Nooks

A. Variety of Book Containers
Within the Classroom Library

B. Students' Book Nooks on Bookshelf
With Book Containers

Photographs by Dianna Dee Damkoehler. Used with permission.

Book covers shown: *The Ultimate Book of Bones* by Jinny Johnson © 1990. Reprinted with permission of Marshall Editions/Quarto Publishing Group. *Mrs. Watson Wants Your Teeth* by Alison McGhee, illustrations copyright © 2004 by Harry Bliss, reproduced by permission of Harcourt, Inc. *Arthur's Thanksgiving* by Marc Brown © 1976. Reprinted with permission of Little, Brown and Company.

However, initially you randomly place books on shelves and into the containers without labels because your students will sort the classroom library themselves. Don't worry about how messy it looks for now. Organization of the books is part of the learning process for your students. Empowering your students with this ongoing task outweighs the initial disarray.

Other items that prove important in terms of organization and management are book nooks and book sticks. A book nook is an individual reader's personal place for self-selected book choices. Book nooks could be made from larger cereal boxes, mailbox cubbies (as in Figure 3), plastic containers, or baskets. A book stick is a management device for your many sorted book containers. For example, we have our students decorate a paint stirring stick. Sizes of these sticks can vary; we get them free by kindly asking the paint expert at our local hardware store. Students use their individual book stick to mark the spot from which they have taken a book. If a student makes a decision to place a book selection in his or her book nook, the book stick is removed as a place holder from the container and is ready to be used again. Book sticks help to maintain the organization of the classroom library by reminding students to return their book to the proper container.

Preparing Your Readers for BOOKMATCH

In any classroom, the first day provides an opportunity to set up learner expectations and establish the tone for the rest of the school year. Routines are introduced as a way to stress their importance. For example, in first grade, time is spent demonstrating how to line up, sit at the carpet, and take turns. This emphasis on learning routines continues for several weeks as the teacher gradually hands over responsibility to students for performing these actions independently. Ideally, you would want to start implementing BOOKMATCH at the beginning of the school year, just as you would implement other vital parts of your grade's curriculum and other daily routines.

The first day of school is the optimal time to present BOOKMATCH to the class, at least visually, by revealing a large BOOKMATCH poster. The poster indicates to your students that BOOKMATCH will be an important

Day one for readers in intermediate grades may include discussion of classroom rules, responsibility of the learners, and classroom arrangement. Establishing the routines will take less time as older students are likely to perform them independently sooner.

part of their day. To make a BOOKMATCH poster, you can use the reproducible version of BOOKMATCH found in the Appendix, enlarge it, and laminate it. You could also use either of the student comment forms found in the Appendix—either the form for primary-grade readers or the form for intermediate-grade readers—simply reproducing the criteria column only. Depending on how large you want your poster, you may choose to have it enlarged at a local copy center.

    You can also access electronic versions of the BOOKMATCH poster as well as the student comment forms for both primary-grade and intermediate-grade readers. Electronic versions of these forms can be found on the website for this book at www.reading.org. You can also purchase a full-color poster and BOOKMATCH bookmarks from www.bookmatchforreaders .com.

CLARIFICATION SPOT

In order to provide a visual of how the students progress through the criteria on the BOOKMATCH poster, we start with a laminated black-and-white copy of the poster and gather nine dry-erase markers of various colors (one for each letter). Each minilesson focusing on a letter of BOOKMATCH criteria begins by coloring in the letter with a new color. This is a great way to draw students' attention to the poster and create a visual association for the criteria already learned.

Getting to Know Your Students

In order to meet the needs of all your students and to differentiate your instruction, you will need to find out more about your students. We suggest "getting to know you" interviews, measuring students' attitudes toward independent reading, and determining students' prior knowledge of self-selection.

"Getting to Know You" Interviews

Interviews are a great way to get to know your students better. Table 5 provides some getting to know you interview questions (Johns & Lenski, 2001) we've used over the years. You may want to choose questions from

TABLE 5
"Getting to Know You" Interview Questions

- Who is in your family?
- What are some things you do together?
- Do you have regular chores or jobs you have to do at home?
- Which indoor/outdoor games do you like?
- What types of collections or hobbies do you have?
- Do you go to any sport practices, music lessons, or clubs?
- Do you have any pets?
- What are your favorite TV programs or movies?
- What is your favorite thing about school?
- What do you like to do in your free time?
- Who are some of your best friends and what do you like to do with them?
- Do you like to play alone?
- What books or magazines do you have at home?
- Do you have a library card?
- Do you go to the library and check books out?
- What is reading?
- What was the last book you read that you REALLY liked?
- What was it about the book that you liked so much?
- Do you like to have someone read to you?
- Do you like to read to others?

- What do you like to read about?
- What was the best book you ever read?
- Do you ever buy books from the store?
- Are there things you are afraid of?
- When you grow up, what do you want to be?
- If you could have three wishes, what would you wish for?
- Have you ever traveled anywhere far away?
- What is something you are really good at?
- What is something you would like to get better at?
- What is something you could teach someone else because you know a lot about it?
- What is your day like after you get home from school?
- What do you think about while you are choosing a book to read?
- If you don't like a book that you are reading, what do you do?
- Have you ever learned something from reading a book?
- Is there anyone at school whom you do not like to be around?

Finish these statements:
- Someday I want to...
- I love it when...
- I can't wait until...

this list and add some of your own. Only you can decide what questions would be most helpful to find out more about your students. We've conducted these interviews in a variety of ways. We have found that the most effective approach with first graders is to have a parent volunteer or other teacher work individually with students. The volunteer reads the interview questions and records the responses. Primary-grade readers may need someone to record responses, but intermediate-grade readers will probably want to write their own responses.

Measuring Students' Attitudes Toward Independent Reading

While getting to know your students, you may choose to measure students' attitudes toward independent reading and book choice through the use of an Independent Reading Attitude Survey. It is important to assess your students' attitudes toward independent reading because their responses expose both negative and positive views from previous experiences at home and in classrooms. As their current teacher, you'll want to understand these attitudes early on so that you can build on the positive and change the negative.

We created our own Independent Reading Attitude Survey by modifying questions or statements most relevant to independent reading on existing surveys (Gambrell, Palmer, Codling, & Mazzoni, 1996; McKenna & Kear, 1990; Tullock-Rhody & Alexander, 1980), and then constructing some additional questions and statements (a reproducible version of the survey can be found in the Appendix). The survey will help you make better decisions when supporting each specific student with BOOKMATCH and as a reader. For example, Figure 4 shows Renee's completed survey. Renee believes that her friend Angela likes to read because "she is always reading." On the other hand, Renee says that the person who doesn't like to read "is barely reading." Renee feels that she is like the person who likes to read; therefore, we want to make sure that we are providing Renee with ample time in school to read. Also, Renee likes the peace of reading alone, but her favorite place to read is at school because she has people to help her when she gets stuck. Offering independent reading during your reading workshop allows all readers to feel as though they are "always reading" and being supported.

The Independent Reading Attitude Survey in this book is just one you can use. There are many other surveys available to learn more about the readers in your classroom. See Johns and Lenski (2001), Routman (2003), and Skolnick (2000) for various surveys and interview options. By assessing your students authentically from the start, you will be able to support their "feelings of efficacy as literacy learners" (Lenski & Nierstheimer, 2004, p. 26).

Later chapters will share how you can use the information gained from the surveys (as well as the interviews and brainstorming sessions described in the sections that follow) to benefit your students. For now, you should administer them and browse them for patterns and responses that catch your attention. We like to create a tally master, showing the

FIGURE 4
Renee's Independent Reading Attitude Survey

A. Front Side of Survey

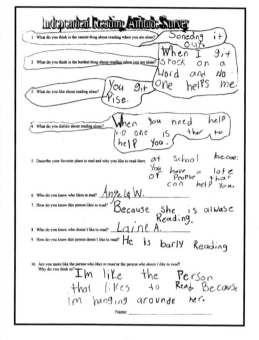

B. Back Side of Survey

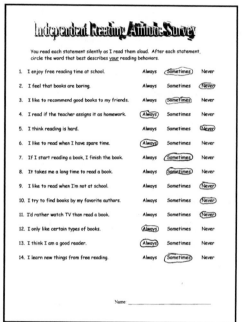

class responses as a whole, and you may wish to do the same. Figure 5 illustrates this tallying of side B on the Independent Reading Attitude Survey. You may find some students will become a high priority for a conference or a guided group based on their responses on the surveys. For example, the tally of Independent Reading Attitude Surveys in Figure 5 reveals that most of these students have a positive attitude about reading, are more apt to read at school than at home, and define themselves as readers. However, the five students who indicated that reading is hard became one of the first guided groups.

Determining Students' Prior Knowledge

Later in this chapter, we will show you how to introduce the concept of just-right books. However, as a way to initially determine the prior

Figure 6 shows Anthony's responses to the Selection Criteria Survey. What these responses tell us is that Anthony has a limited understanding of self-selecting just-right books. Like many readers, he is thinking about books on a surface level. However, in order for him to dig deeper into books and to find books that he will finish, he'll need to think about more than the three criteria he marked as "sometimes": the length of the book, how hard the words are, and how he relates to the book. As with the Independent Reading Attitude Survey, you may want to tally all Selection Criteria Surveys to look for patterns across the group and responses that catch your attention. Figure 7 illustrates this whole-class tallying of student responses. On this Selection Criteria Survey tally sheet, eight students indicated that they do not look at how difficult the words are. These eight students were also called for a guided group in the first few days of reading workshop. Because of the surveys, there was a clear

FIGURE 6
Anthony's Selection Criteria Survey

SELECTION CRITERIA SURVEY

	Always	Sometimes	Never	I don't know
Do I think about how long the book is?		☒		
Do I think about the style of writing? Does it sound like talk?			☒	☒
Do I think about how the book is organized?				☒
Do I think about how much I already know about the topic of the book?			☒	
Do I think about how hard the words are?		☒		
Do I think about the genre, or what type of book it is?				☒
Do I think about how comfortable I am with the topic of the book?			☒	
Do I think about how I can relate to the book?		☒		
Do I think about how interested I am in the topic, or author, or illustrator?				☒

	Always 5	Usually 4	Sometimes 3	Rarely 2	Never 1
How often do I finish a book I select?			☑		

What are some reasons why I might not finish a book I start reading?

Kas I Dot Lik It,

FIGURE 5
Whole-Class Tally of Responses to Indeper
Reading Attitude Survey

Independent Reading Attitude Survey
You read each statement silently as I read them aloud. After each statement, circle the word that best describes your reading behaviors.

1. I enjoy free reading time at school.
   Always — Sometimes — Never

2. I feel that books are boring.
   Always — Sometimes — Never

3. I like to recommend good books to my friends.
   Always — Sometimes — Never

4. I read if the teacher assigns it as homework.
   Always — Sometimes — Never

5. I think reading is hard.
   Always — Sometimes — Never

6. I like to read when I have spare time.
   Always — Sometimes — Never

7. If I start reading a book, I finish the book.
   Always — Sometimes — Never

8. It takes me a long time to read a book.
   Always — Sometimes — Never

9. I like to read when I'm not at school.
   Always — Sometimes — Never

10. I try to find books by my favorite authors.
    Always — Sometimes — Never

11. I'd rather watch TV than read a book.
    Always — Sometimes — Never

12. I only like certain types of books.
    Always — Sometimes — Never

13. I think I am a good reader.
    Always — Sometimes — Never

14. I learn new things from free reading.
    Always — Sometimes — Never

knowledge that your students bring to the classroom regarding cho books and knowing that a book is just right, we suggest using the Selection Criteria Survey (see the Appendix for a reproducible versi the survey). This survey will let you inside the mind of each individu and the students' responses will help later in guiding your instructio BOOKMATCH and independent reading time.

There are two purposes behind the Selection Criteria Survey. The to find out which book-selection criteria, if any, are currently being use each student in your class. The second reason is to gather information a why students might be abandoning—not finishing—books that they ha chosen by themselves. A whole-group session in which each student spr out within the room with a clipboard, a pencil, and a survey can help yo gather information quickly. You should read each question aloud, provid enough time for the students to think about the question and respond.

FIGURE 7

FIGURE 7
Whole-Class Tally of Responses to Selection Criteria Survey

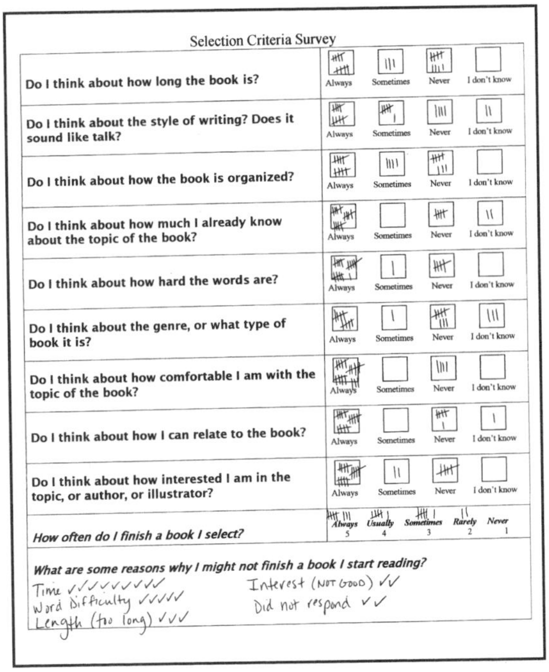

Selection Criteria Survey

Question	Always	Sometimes	Never	I don't know
Do I think about how long the book is?	卌 卌	|||	卌 ||||	
Do I think about the style of writing? Does it sound like talk?	卌 卌	卌	|||	||
Do I think about how the book is organized?	卌 卌	||||	卌 |||	
Do I think about how much I already know about the topic of the book?	卌 卌 卌		卌	||
Do I think about how hard the words are?	卌 卌 卌			卌	
Do I think about the genre, or what type of book it is?	卌 卌			卌 |||	|||
Do I think about how comfortable I am with the topic of the book?	卌 卌 卌		|||	
Do I think about how I can relate to the book?	卌 卌 卌		卌			
Do I think about how interested I am in the topic, or author, or illustrator?	卌 卌 卌	||	卌	

How often do I finish a book I select?	卌 |||	卌		卌		||	
	Always 5	Usually 4	Sometimes 3	Rarely 2	Never 1

What are some reasons why I might not finish a book I start reading?

Time ✓✓✓✓✓✓✓✓ Interest (NOT Good) ✓✓
Word Difficulty ✓✓✓✓✓ Did not respond ✓✓
Length (too long) ✓✓✓

purpose to the guided groups—showing them how to open a book to any page and read aloud to check the text for difficulty.

Seeing Your Students as Capable Readers

It is important for teachers to see their students as capable readers. The term *capable* means that regardless of their background knowledge and their previous experiences with reading and self-selection, all students have the ability to be successful independent readers. Each student will need various levels of support and experiences. The framework shown in Figure 8 illustrates how students begin the school year as capable learners before they become increasingly responsible for using self-selection strategies according to our pattern of implementing BOOKMATCH. This pattern identifies the Phases of Learning students experience as they progress through a full school

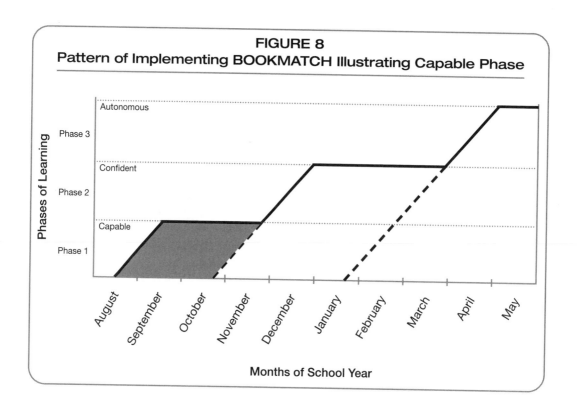

FIGURE 8
Pattern of Implementing BOOKMATCH Illustrating Capable Phase

Phases of Learning

Phase 3 — Autonomous

Phase 2 — Confident

Phase 1 — Capable

August · September · October · November · December · January · February · March · April · May

Months of School Year

year of practicing and refining the acts of self-selection and independent reading. As students move through Phase 1, we see them as capable.

Capable readers can move through the capable phase to the confident phase when they experience feelings of self-efficacy within the reading workshop. Students need to know that their teachers believe that readers need choice, that readers can think meaningfully about text found in the classroom library, that readers can remain engaged during independent reading time, and that readers have a variety of reading preferences. When your students acquire a reading identity that is defined by choice, meaningful thinking about text, increased engagement during reading, and an awareness of their own preferences, they have reached the confident phase. Through your own observations, responses, and think-alouds, you will provide the support needed for your readers to experience this success. From August through at least October, you can expect your students to be in the capable phase, until independent reading routines are well established, leading to more confident behaviors and a "gradual release of responsibility" (Pearson & Gallagher, 1983; Routman, 2003).

Sometime during the first week, you will begin the independent reading routine with these capable learners. In order to prepare your students, you must be prepared yourself. Start by defining what a reader does by asking yourself these questions:

- How do I select a book?
- What kinds of books do I like to read?
- What topics hold my interest?
- When do I like to read most?
- Do I have favorite authors?
- What motivates me to read?
- When do I decide to commit to a book?
- Why might I abandon a book?

Thinking about what you do as a reader will prepare you for the reading behaviors your students will demonstrate. We really want you to think long and hard about the above questions because chances are the way you answer them will shape how you define and model what a reader is to your students. This is your belief system about independent reading. If you were to ask these same questions to a friend or someone you view as a reader, would he or she respond in the same way? Probably not. Your students will not all respond the same way either. The students in your classroom are capable and will exhibit similar reading behaviors, such as page turning, looking at the cover, skimming text, enjoying illustrations, and abandoning. However, because they are in the early phase of learning the process of self-selection, these behaviors may seem exaggerated to you because you already have the skills and defined preferences for successful book selection. You need to be tolerant of these exaggerated behaviors as students move through the selection process themselves.

At the same time students demonstrate these reading behaviors, they also define themselves as readers and learn their own preferences. This is why you need to recognize that each reader is unique and their behaviors and preferences should be celebrated within your reading workshop. Readers' preferences should be appreciated and considered in the students' development of self-efficacy. One thing we know is that readers need the feeling of being able to succeed. We want them to see that *their* preferences are validated. Your role as a reader and as a teacher will be to get this message across.

You will also need to consider your students' previous experiences and background knowledge. These experiences develop each student's schema. According to Anderson and Pearson (1984), "a schema is an abstract knowledge structure" (p. 259). These knowledge structures resemble a network of connected components and are stored in memory and retrieved during the act of reading to make sense of the text. Our memories, then, are structured more like a thesaurus than a dictionary (Pearson, 1982), for more efficient retrieval. A reader will select appropriate schema from his or her memories based on background experiences and textual clues. For example, Anna (all student names are pseudonyms) is a first grader who has traveled more places than some adults. Anna demonstrates typical first-grade reading behaviors, but has a strong vocabulary because she is often engaged in dialogue with her parents and other adults. When Anna selects books in the classroom library about another country or state, we're comfortable knowing that these are topics for which she has the appropriate schema for understanding. We also know from conferences with Anna that she will seek out answers for something she doesn't understand.

Schema also plays a significant role in each student's ability to succeed at more difficult texts. For example, first grader Brock knows all about space. He is our resident expert on the topic and often teaches others in the classroom about it. His bedroom at home has been transformed into the solar system. He has visited museums, watched movies, and read all the space books in the classroom library. Brock has developed a sophisticated schema that supports his ability to gain meaning from complex texts on space, which most first graders would not be able to read. However, if Brock attempted to read and construct meaning from a complex text about a different topic, he might not be successful. This is because Brock may not have extensive knowledge about other topics stored as schema that he can draw upon.

Like Brock, all readers organize their experiences into categories and retrieve the necessary information to construct meaning based on the topic, text difficulty, and their connections to the text. The organization and categorical structure of BOOKMATCH supports students' development of what Piaget calls the biological or natural tendency of organization (cited in Crain, 2000). Cognitively, elementary students (even first graders) are capable of selecting their own books, defining their preferences, thinking about their reading process, reflecting on their growth as readers, sustaining engagement during independent reading time, and sharing their knowledge with others. A review of the cognitive development theories of Piaget (1973), Vygotsky (1978), and Wolfe (2001) suggests that children inherently organize objects into categories and get more sophisticated in their classifications from interactions with texts, their participation in culture, and their interactions with more capable peers or adult masters. A review of reading behaviors and developmental stages suggests that "young readers and writers are believed to engage in the same types of literacy processes, though at a less sophisticated level, as those used by older children and adults" (Lenski & Nierstheimer, 2004, p. 47). One literacy process in which readers engage is organizing books into categories. We refer to this as sorting.

Immersing in Sorting: The Start of Independent Reading

We want students to take ownership of the classroom library and its organization. Therefore, sorting becomes an opportunity for students to browse many books of varying difficulties, topics, and genres and then organize these books into categories decided upon by the students. Through browsing, students have the opportunity to handle books, look through books, and familiarize themselves with the topics of available books in the classroom library. By sorting those books, students are able to take ownership of their library through the process of categorizing these books into groups. During independent reading the students share the role of sorting as a way to fill the library with books for self-selection: "The student-involved classroom library process increases the number of books children choose from their classroom library" (Jones, 2006, p. 576). This sense of ownership is illustrated in Figure 9, a drawing of our classroom library created by one of our students, Alysse. This drawing showed up on Jessica's desk one day, confirming that the process of sorting and labeling containers was a meaningful experience for this student.

Begin by laying out books on the tables or desks of your students. We generally did this first thing in the morning on the first day of school to create a book experience right away. In order to be prepared you could spread out the books the night before. Based on the needs of your

FIGURE 9
Alysse's Drawing of Classroom Library

students, you may choose to let them spend several days just browsing books before adding the task of sorting.

We make sure to put out books that we guess will be of interest, like books in the Arthur series by Marc Brown, books about school, authors studied the year before, poetry collections, picture books with large print and repetitive language, books about friends, and animal books. This is

 TIPS FOR INTERMEDIATE-GRADE READERS

If more than one class of students works with your classroom library, you will need to adapt the process of sorting. Initially, a class will sort a portion of the library and create temporary labels using sticky notes so that all users of the library have an opportunity to voice their opinions. The temporary label allows other students (or classes) to add their own sticky notes and suggestions as they question the reasoning behind the initial decisions. Because texts for intermediate readers may not provide graphic clues like picture books, your students will make more informed decisions, taking into consideration their previous experiences with authors, genres, preferences, and topics. There will be more conversation among students as they think through appropriate groupings for the books. A final step of taking ownership in this process will be determining a permanent label for each container.

your first chance during the school year to spark interest in books and reading with the whole group. Students should be told at this time to talk with their peers about how the books on the tables might be sorted. Davis (2005) shares how "conversation allows students to be reflective about their reading as they familiarize themselves with what books are available to read" (p. 4). After just a few minutes, students will have more than one book that can go in the same group. This is the start of your sorted classroom library. As a teacher you will support this meaningful and necessary shared experience in a nonjudgmental way, going with the students' thoughts and seeing things through the eyes of your readers. The following dialogue shares how you as the teacher may initiate the sorting process.

Teacher: Now we need to sort these books into our library so we can find them easily. Let's find books that go together. Look at this table, there is a book about a dog.

Jimmy: I have a book about a dog, too.

Teacher: Yes, does anyone else have a book about a dog? [grabs an empty container] These books go together. [shows students how to place the two dog books in the container] All dog books go here.

Students start browsing the books at their tables and place dog books into the container. Eventually, students notice other topics or themes of the books and begin voicing their ideas for other containers.

Emma: I have spooky books.

Teacher: [notices Emma's book is a Halloween book] Oh, Halloween, books about ghosts, books where characters are scared. [grabs another container and students look for more spooky books] All spooky books go here.

Sorting of the books continues in this manner but starts to happen very rapidly. Some students will take control of their own containers and tell other students where to put certain topics. For example, Laine calls out, "Tree books in here!" This is a good time for you to step back and let students have more control over the container topics.

CLARIFICATION SPOT

For time purposes, recap the types of containers that were created in the first session and tell students the central location for books that still need to be sorted. Unsorted books remain off limits until they have been placed in a container.

On subsequent days, after a minilesson based on BOOKMATCH, students continue to browse books spread out on tables. Some tables start with a filled container from a previous day's sorting rather than unsorted books. Students with the filled container will use a blank piece of paper and markers to create the container label, as illustrated in Figure 10. Other students continue to sort books. Labels made by the students are an important component of sorting and setting up the library. Paper, markers, and clear packaging tape will help make sturdy labels.

The process of sorting the library may take a couple of months, usually through to October. For a class that is not familiar with browsing and sorting books, you may want to begin by presorting books so that students can more easily make categories and all books have a place. For example, you could create a few obvious categories, such as Arthur books, nonfiction and fiction books about a certain animal, and books on snow.

FIGURE 10
Student Creating a Container Label

Photograph by Dianna Dee Damkoehler. Used with permission.

With only those categories available at their tables, you are providing an opportunity for students to successfully and accurately sort the books, but still do it "on their own." Once students become better at sorting, this level of scaffolding should be removed.

You may notice that some containers will begin to overflow. For example, our Animals container was bursting at the seams (see Figure 11A). This overflowing container creates a purpose for more complex instruction about genre. The class was ready to examine that particular text set and see how those books could be further sorted. We guided the students toward sorting the container into fiction and nonfiction because

---

FIGURE 11
Overflowing Containers Resulting From the Sorting Process

A. Overflowing Container With Books Sorted Into "Animals" Category

B. Teacher Conducting Whole-Group Minilesson With an Overflowing Container

Photographs by Dianna Dee Damkoehler. Used with permission.

these terms are a way to initiate conversations about genre (see Figure 11B). The following script shares this lesson.

> I'm having you sit in a circle today because I want you to really be able to see this Animals container that we've created. This container looks really full to me. I'm worried because we still have many other books that need to be sorted, and this container won't hold anymore. Is there a way that we can sort the books from this container to create even more containers? As I lay them out [teacher begins scattering books one at a time in the center of the circle], I want you to be looking very closely at the names of the books, at the book covers, at the different animals you see, and also what type of books they are. Really look closely. Are these books about pretend animals or animals that are not real? These books are called fiction books. Or, are they books about real animals or facts about real animals? These books are called nonfiction books...

This lesson continued as students worked through the separation and resorting of the Animals container. They ended up with two containers: Animals Fiction and Animals Nonfiction. Later in the year, we were able to expand their understanding of genre by further sorting fiction and nonfiction into the common categories found in other libraries, such as mammals, mysteries, biographies, and so on. These additional lessons can occur as needed throughout the school year.

Your First BOOKMATCH Lessons: Introducing Students to the Self-Selection Process

Because browsing and sorting are such important parts of learning self-selection, your first lesson with BOOKMATCH really begins when you first explain browsing and sorting. Therefore, you'll probably want to make sure your students have had some opportunity to practice browsing and sorting books before you begin your first minilessons about BOOKMATCH. Because some sorting has already taken place, there could be some books displayed on shelves, in some previously sorted containers, on spinning racks, and of course on their tables. Then, additional minilessons are conducted in addition to the already established routine of browsing and sorting. Together, these lessons and browsing and sorting take place within the first few weeks of the school year. Based on the needs of your students, you may decide to combine some of these lessons into one or break them down even more and spread them out over a few days while your students continue to browse and sort the classroom library.

Your first minilesson is to empower your students by introducing them to the concept of an independent reader. To set your students up as the capable learners they are, hold a morning meeting to share what readers do during independent reading. From this point forward, you will refer to your students as readers. You need to encourage students to define themselves as readers, too. The most important factor for independent reading success is the teacher's attitude (Gardiner, 2005). Therefore, you need to be excited and energetic in your interactions with students and let them know that you value their differences. At this point, you are telling the students that they are independent readers. Independent readers choose books on their own, read the books they choose, and use strategies with unknown words while continuing to challenge themselves. Because they are independent readers, you'll entice them with the meaning of the word *independent* and tell them that they *get* to do those things by themselves, and they *get* to do those things every day. This empowerment helps them progress through the phases of learning.

Your second minilesson is actually a whole-group brainstorming session about the main criteria used by your students when choosing books for independent reading. We suggest the following leading questions to help the brainstorming process:

- What is a just-right book?
- How do you know you have a book that is right for you as a reader?
- What do you do when you choose a just-right book?
- What do you think about when you choose a just-right book?
- How do you know a book is *not* just right?

Figure 12 shares the responses from a brainstorming session in a first-grade classroom.

You may be surprised by the responses, noticing gaps or possibly greater knowledge than expected. Many of your students will indicate some awareness of how to choose a book. However, this is where you dig

> 8/26/05
> What criteria do we
> use to choose a book?
> How do we choose books?
> • looks like a good book
> • looking at the pictures
> • look at the cover
> • hear others reading that book
> • look for a specific illustrator
> • look inside the book at the words
>   the words might sound good
> • you read some of it
> • if I want to learn about the
>   stuff it teaches
> • read the title
> • the words look good by the author
>
> • might look funny
>
> • if you can read the title,
>   you can probably read the book
> • think about the movie
> • you already read the book

Photograph by R. Lynn Harrison. Used with permission.

deeper for true understanding. For example, when a student of ours gave the response, "If you can read the title, you can probably read the book," it was obvious that more work was needed, especially at the individual level. The brainstorming session will be incredibly revealing of where your students are as a whole group, but the activity will only let you inside the minds of those who choose to participate (see page 24 on determining students' prior knowledge by using the Selection Criteria Survey).

Your third minilesson introduces the concept of BOOKMATCH. Write BOOK and MATCH on the board and talk to the readers in your class about how they are going be a part of something very special that readers do. Show them how you can put the words together to make the new term BOOKMATCH. Tell them that you will teach them how to make a book match and how to choose a just-right book. Draw attention to the BOOKMATCH poster, and keep this initial exposure to BOOKMATCH brief. Depending on the readiness of your students, you may choose to explain more or simply wait until the next day of lessons about BOOKMATCH to continue.

The following script demonstrates a fourth minilesson on how you can use modeling with a think-aloud for your students.

> I want you to watch because I'm going to show you how I find a book for myself that is just right. Yesterday I showed you this poster and talked with you about BOOKMATCH. BOOKMATCH is a tool for readers. It's like a construction worker who has a belt and needs a hammer. Construction workers need that tool to do their job. Well, you're a reader. That's your job. And as a reader you need a tool that helps you pick out a book that is perfect for you. That's what BOOKMATCH is. Anna might go into the library, open a book, and decide this is not the book she wants to read and put it down. And right after her, Peter might pick up that same book and say, "I love this book." We are all different learners, and we are all different readers. There are so many books in our library that we are going to need a tool to help us choose just-right books. As you go off today to browse books, think about which books seem just right for you.

The following day, your fifth minilesson should begin to focus on the criteria of BOOKMATCH and how this tool will help them find just-right books, as illustrated in the following script:

> Take a look at B, which stands for book length. [teacher should be pointing to the B on the poster] What should I think about when I'm talking about book length? [teacher should model how a reader does this by turning pages in a book] What do you think I'm thinking about? As I turn the pages, I'm thinking to myself, is this book too long? Too short? Or, is it just right? I also need to think about myself as a reader. If I feel like the book is too long, I'm not going to choose it today. If I feel it is too short, then I can't really learn new things or be a thinker. I'll know a book is just right when I feel comfortable and ready to commit. What I mean is that I think this is the best choice for me, and I like the choice I made. When I feel good about the length, I've thought about B and I am on my way to a book match.

At this point, you will have increased students' exposure to BOOKMATCH and started the thinking process about self-selection. Your modeling is the key to your students' understanding. To wrap up this

TIPS FOR INTERMEDIATE-GRADE READERS

Although it's possible to teach all the letters of BOOKMATCH in one minilesson, we do not recommend this approach, even for advanced readers. Thinking through all nine criteria at the same time as a first experience may be so overwhelming that students revert to ineffective selection behaviors out of frustration. On the other hand, more advanced readers will be able to focus their attention on more than one criterion, so you will need to find the balance between the amount of information you present and your students' previous book-selection experiences.

minilesson and continue the learning process, you should use a transition to move your readers from whole-group to individual practice.

The following dialogue is an example of how you would facilitate a transition after teaching about the letter *B*—book length.

Teacher:	[with the students still at the carpet, the teacher begins the transition] If you feel like you understand book length, show me a thumbs up. [this provides a quick assessment of who understood the minilesson] Now you are going to go to your tables to browse books and practice finding a book with just-right length. But first, I want you to tell me what you can think about when you are trying to make a book match.
Leah:	How long it is.
Teacher:	That's right, you think about how long it is. Off you go. Matthew?
Matthew:	Or how short it is.
Teacher:	That's right, you think about how short the book might be. Off you go. Lisa?
Lisa:	You turn the pages.
Teacher:	Yes, Lisa. You should turn the pages and be thinking about how long the book is, and then think if the length of the book is good for you. Off you go. Joe?
Joe:	Oh! How long it is.
Teacher:	You're right. You're really thinking. That's what Leah is going to think about, too. Good readers will think about

how long the book is when trying to make a book match…

After the transition, students will spend about 10 minutes browsing all the books at their tables to evaluate the length (see Figure 13). Their task is to find one book that matches their preference for book length. This is a sharing time, so there will be student discussion and even excitement about new books they discover. Let this happen naturally, as social interaction is a part of learning (Erikson, as cited in Crain, 2000; Vygotsky, 1978; Piaget, as cited in Woolfolk, 2000). To assess and wrap up this activity, you could ask students if anyone has found a book that is a good match for length, using the following sample prompts.

FIGURE 13
Readers Browsing Books on Tabletops

Photograph by Dianna Dee Damkoehler. Used with permission.

Book cover from *Go Away, Big Green Monster* by Edward R. Emberley © 1992. Reprinted with permission from Little, Brown and Company.

- Did anyone find a book that is way too long?
- Did anyone find a book that is too short?
- How many found a book that is just right?
- If you found a book that is just the right length for you, and you think you might want to look at it more, go put that book in your book nook now.

Another way to wrap up the lesson could be to have students categorize their books into piles of too-long, just-right, and too-short lengths. Students would then discuss and justify their categorization.

Most students probably won't match themselves to a book during this fifth lesson because it is their first experience selecting a just-right book while using BOOKMATCH, but you always need to provide the opportunity to practice what you just modeled for them. Although your demonstration about the criterion of book length is over, you should allow students additional time to browse the books. Many readers will actually engage in a text and begin using the behaviors they will be expected to exhibit during independent reading time. For nonreaders, these behaviors may reflect limited literacy experiences; however, we can't deny them this much needed opportunity to learn and develop as readers. Sometimes we expect students to be experts too soon.

The Importance of Transitioning From Whole-Group to Individual Practice

It is important to make a transition similar to the one in the fifth minilesson before you send students off for individual practice of any minilesson skill. The purpose of this transition is to encourage students to verbalize their understandings of parts of the BOOKMATCH minilesson. Some students may repeat another's responses. Allow all students, one at

PARENT CONNECTION

You will want to prepare a letter that explains BOOKMATCH within reading workshop. This can be sent home after you introduce BOOKMATCH and begin your initial lessons. A sample letter is presented in Figure 14.

FIGURE 14
Sample Letter to Parents Introducing BOOKMATCH

Dear Parents,

Attached you will find a BOOKMATCH poster that we use during our independent reading time. It is a list of questions and criteria that your child can think about when choosing a book for independent reading time. We are learning each letter of BOOKMATCH and will have time to think about these questions with regard to a specific book of our choice.

We will continue to practice using BOOKMATCH as we browse and self-select books from the classroom library and the school library. The questions help us think about whether we have a just-right book. Sometimes, we find we need to abandon the book or choose a different one. This is a perfectly acceptable reading behavior. As your child reads books independently at home, from the public library or from your own collection, please allow him or her to practice using BOOKMATCH, thinking about the questions, and talking to you to confirm whether or not it is a just-right book.

Thank you for the continued support of your child as a reader.

Sincerely,

Teacher's Name

a time, to verbalize how they will apply the minilesson during independent reading.

From the many works of Lucy Calkins, Donald Graves, Shelley Harwayne, Sharon Taberski, Regie Routman, and others, we have come to understand the effectiveness of telling students how smart their thinking is. We like to make sure they, too, believe they are capable. They need to feel that they "already possess an understanding and wisdom that resides deep within" (Skolnick, 2000, p. 91). In the example used for the fifth minilesson (see page 40), you can see how the teacher provides the opportunity to employ a skill in the completion of the assigned task, building students' sense of competence.

The following are some additional transition ideas that can be meaningful while providing opportunities for quick assessments:

- Reader names a criterion from BOOKMATCH that he or she already uses.
- Reader names a criterion from BOOKMATCH that he or she will try for the first time today.
- Reader models the use of a criterion from BOOKMATCH with book in hand.

The transition could also begin with students on the carpet with their own books. After listening to a teacher read-aloud and minilesson, readers could use their books to transition in one of the following ways:

- Reader shares a criterion that he or she is comfortable using.
- Reader tells in his or her own words why a specific book is just right.
- Reader shares the purpose for reading that specific book today.

In this chapter, we've presented ways for you to get started with BOOKMATCH. We suggested preparing your classroom, getting to know your students, and preparing your readers. Through five minilessons, we've stressed the importance of modeling and introduced you to the concept of transitioning. In the next chapter, you will learn more about transitioning and the flow of activity that will occur during your reading workshop and specifically independent reading time.

Reflection Point

Before reading more about the implementation and use of BOOKMATCH with your own students, please take the time to think about the following:

- your capable readers
- just-right books
- the flow of activity during your literacy time

In what ways have these practices affected your mind-set about literacy learners?

CHAPTER 3

Implementing BOOKMATCH: Moving Capable Readers to Confidence

"If we want children to develop habits that readers keep, we must heighten their awareness by explicitly modeling and pointing out what it is that readers do and giving them time to practice these behaviors in authentic situations using real books."

—Debbie Miller, *Reading With Meaning: Teaching Comprehension in the Primary Grades*

An optimal reading workshop environment is one in which there is a well-established routine. This routine becomes part of your schedule and takes on a natural flow. Now that you have had the opportunity to prepare your classroom, get to know your students, and prepare your readers for BOOKMATCH with introductory lessons, this routine can be established. In this chapter we will build on the flow of activity during reading workshop as we give examples of demonstrations through think-alouds, minilessons, verbal prompts, transitions, and practice. With modeling at the forefront and a clear understanding of the developmental abilities of your readers, you can explicitly demonstrate necessary strategies for the independent self-selection of just-right books. In this chapter, we will also share a variety of focused BOOKMATCH lessons and introduce the concept of abandoning and what to do when a book doesn't fit. Furthermore, these lessons and experiences within the flow of

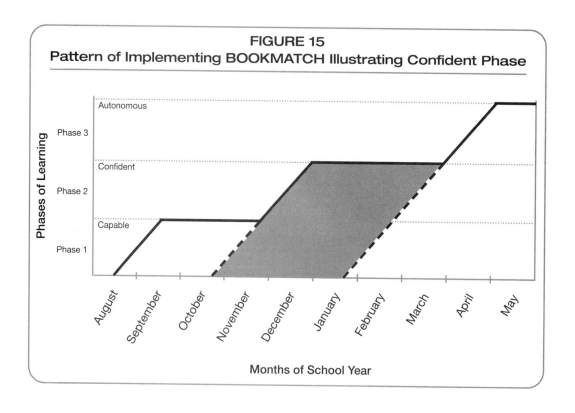

FIGURE 15
Pattern of Implementing BOOKMATCH Illustrating Confident Phase

activity will move your students from the capable phase to the confident phase within the pattern of implementing BOOKMATCH (see Figure 15).

Establishing the Flow of Activity for Your Readers: What to Expect

Although you will spend the first few months of the school year modeling and preparing students for independence, your objective is to reach a natural flow of activity that successfully encompasses all components of reading workshop. Your students will develop the ability to choose just-right books and their time spent reading will increase. We promise. When they're ready, students will voluntarily choose a new book. That's when the phrase, "Wow, I see so many readers doing what good readers do," is no longer just encouragement, but honest praise.

Let's look ahead to October, when the flow of activity within your classroom will be well established (see Figure 16). The flow of activity begins with whole-group instruction of a read-aloud with a clear purpose

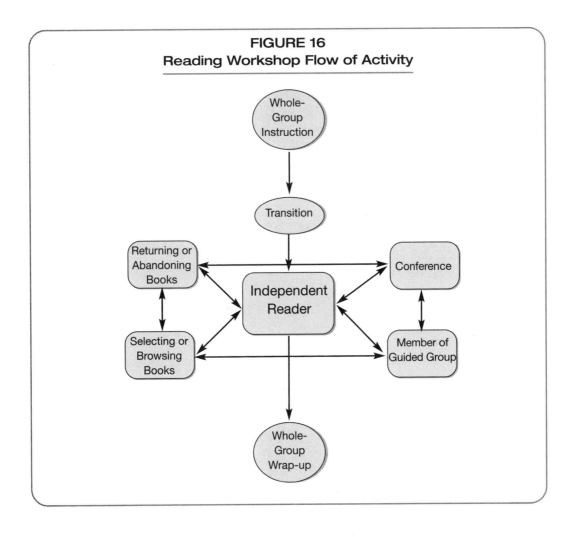

FIGURE 16
Reading Workshop Flow of Activity

Whole-Group Instruction

Transition

Returning or Abandoning Books

Conference

Independent Reader

Selecting or Browsing Books

Member of Guided Group

Whole-Group Wrap-up

in mind, such as introducing a new BOOKMATCH criterion. After discussion, students are asked to describe what they might think about when choosing a book that day. This is a way to help your students make the transition to independent reading. Students one by one move from the carpet to the classroom library, getting books from their book nooks or using their book stick to make a self-selection. Students then return to their seats to read. Notice from Figure 16 that many literacy events take place simultaneously during this independent portion of the reading workshop. Being an independent reader involves selecting and browsing books, returning and abandoning books, participating in a conference, and being a member of a guided group.

You will now make instructional decisions to call a small guided group or work with an individual reader. The small group of students would have some form of a guided lesson lasting no more than 10 minutes. In this teacher-led experience, students may receive explicit instruction based on various needs. During these guided groups, (or when working with an individual reader) we do not allow other students to interrupt. The following are some common purposes for a guided group:

- Making meaning from print
- Analyzing text
- Discussing genre elements
- Sorting
- Practicing fluency
- Taking a picture walk
- Applying reading strategies

All other students remain engaged as independent readers and when necessary (based on their own needs), return books to the classroom library and choose new books. Your focus can remain on the small group or individual student because all other students are capable of making their own decisions as readers. When you're finished, the students from the small group can go back to being independent readers who make their own choices.

Students should be verbally praised for what they do well as readers and given the option to spread out within the room, selecting comfortable chairs, the floor, or different tables as their reading location. However, we control who spreads out by recognizing those students who are doing what good readers do. The purpose of this verbal praise is to reinforce and expand students' independent behaviors. Table 6 provides some statements of praise to verbalize what you see during reading workshop.

At the conclusion of independent reading, there is a whole-group wrap-up in which readers share what went well for them during reading workshop time with regard to reading strategies and selection strategies. Early on, you will have to describe what went well and tell what you noticed

TABLE 6
Statements of Praise

- Wow! Look at these readers!
- We need to do the reader dance.
- I am so impressed by what I see.
- You're doing what good readers do_____ [student name]. You may spread out to a comfy chair.
- Keep it up!
- I see readers really looking at the words.
- I see readers using strategies.
- I see readers that have found just-right books.
- Look at how _____ is turning the pages of the book and thinking about the length and the way the book is organized.
- _____, you need to share with the class how this book is a BOOKMATCH for you.
- _____, you seem so interested in your book. Share what went well for you.
- It's time to give each other compliments as readers. Who would like to start?
- _____ just mentioned that this book would be a great read-aloud because....
- I think it is amazing the way you think about one another as readers and what might interest each of us.

regarding students' using strategies for self-selection. Eventually, this modeling will lead to a wrap-up that more closely resembles a conversation with interaction among all participants. Sometimes this is done at students' tables, other times we get better overall attention and sincere listening when we move to the carpet to share. Students will look forward to this moment as they will have self-selection strategies to show off. To get the dialogue started we use several prompts, such as the following:

What went well today for you as a reader?

Who made a book match today?

Turn and talk to your neighbor about....

Share with someone at your table about a connection you made from your reading.

Share one reason why the book you have is just right for you.

Skolnick (2000) reminds us, "Sharing work in a respectful circle of peers nudges routine requirements to a deeper level of commitment. Like a high tide raises all boats, group enthusiasm and support raise the level of effort and desire to achieve" (p. 33). Praise is given to peers by peers, and often, we are so pleased with the independent reading time that we get up to do the "reader dance." The reader dance is when we all turn around in unison and then turn back the other way while chanting, "Go, first grade! Go, first grade! We're readers! We're readers!" Everyone always enjoys the reader dance, as it is a sure sign of success had by all that day. The independent reading time of your reading workshop should follow the same schedule each day.

Following the celebration and wrap-up is an opportune time for students to fill out a reading log, showing what was read that day. Figure 17 shows two examples of reading logs that we have used with first graders. Both these logs are simple, open-ended, and provide documentation of students' responses to their self-selections. Examples of both can be found in the Appendix. Additionally, Figure 17B allows space for the teacher's running record of the student's oral reading that could be used during a

FIGURE 17
Reading Response Logs

A. Susan's Reading Log

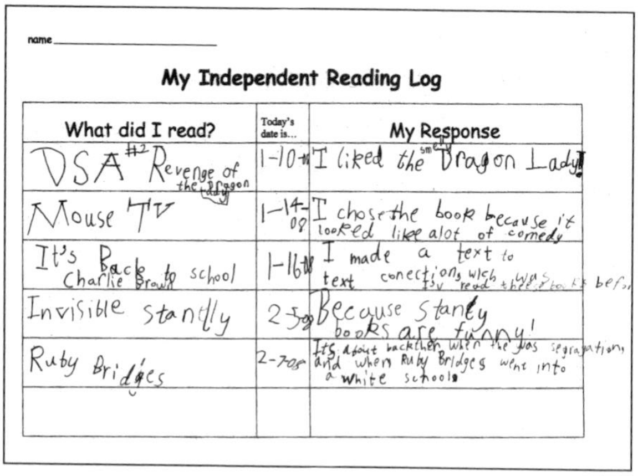
name

My Independent Reading Log

What did I read?	Today's date is...	My Response
DSA #2 Revenge of the Dragon Lady	1-10-08	I liked the Dragon Lady!
Mouse TV	1-14-08	I chose the book because it looked like alot of comedy
It's Back to school Charlie Brown	1-16-08	I made a text to text conections wich I've read the story before
Invisible stanlly	2-5-08	Because stanly books are funny!
Ruby Bridges	2-7-08	Its about back then when there was segragation, and when Ruby Bridges went into a white school

B. Gunnar's Reading Log

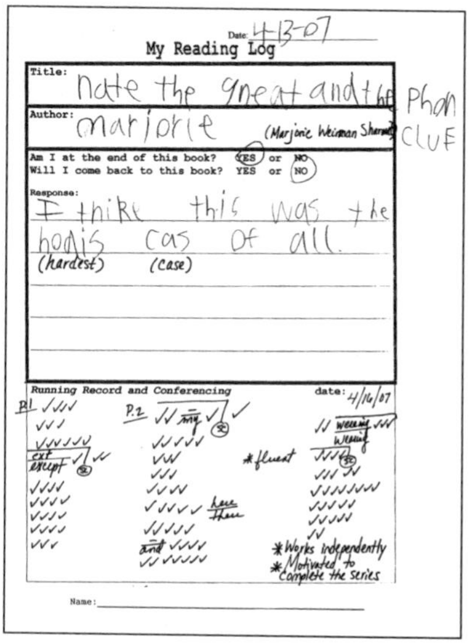
Date: 4-13-07

My Reading Log

Title: nate the great and the Phon CLUE

Author: marjorie (Marjorie Weinman Sharmat)

Am I at the end of this book? YES or NO
Will I come back to this book? YES or NO

Response: I thike this was the hodis cas of all. (hardest) (case)

Running Record and Conferencing date: 4/16/07

*fluent
*Works independently
*Motivated to complete the series

Name:

reading conference. The results of the running record indicate whether the student has selected a just-right book. We recommend waiting until after the independent reading time to have students fill out these reading logs so as not to take time away from reading.

Continuing BOOKMATCH Lessons

Your first lessons with BOOKMATCH, presented in Chapter 2, introduce critical concepts like browsing, sorting, transitions, independent readers, and BOOKMATCH. We also shared how we taught *B—book length*. This section presents a model minilesson for introducing *K—knowledge prior to book*, along with lesson starters for the rest of the BOOKMATCH criteria. Table 3 in Chapter 1 on breaking down BOOKMATCH also provides information that you can use for presenting each criterion.

It's a good idea to start with book length, manageable text, connection, and high-interest, because these are generally the criteria with which students have had previous experiences.

A Model Minilesson on K—Knowledge Prior to Book

At this point, students are doing exactly what you've taught them and are really thinking about books in new ways. You will also begin to think about books in new ways, leading to authentic demonstrations. For example, while preparing to teach the concept of sense of self, Jessica wanted to use *Arthur's Nose* by Marc Brown (2001) as a read-aloud (see Figure 18A). If you are not familiar with this book, it is one of the original Arthur books with very different looking characters than those your students may know. Jessica realized it would be the perfect book to introduce *K—knowledge prior to book*, as she demonstrates here:

> Today I'm going to show you how I think about *K—knowledge prior to book*, before I make a selection. [you should be pointing to the word *Knowledge* on the poster] When I think about knowledge about the book, I might ask myself these questions. [you should run a finger under the words as you read] What do I already know about this topic, this book, or this author? I picked up this book called *Arthur's Nose* [hold up the book] and I think I might already know something about this book because I recognize the name Marc Brown. I know that Marc Brown writes the Arthur books, but this

FIGURE 18
Books Used for BOOKMATCH Minilessons

A. Cover for *Arthur's Nose* Used in Minilesson on *K*—Knowledge Prior to Book

B. Cover for *Arthur's Tooth* Used in Minilesson on *K*—Knowledge Prior to Book

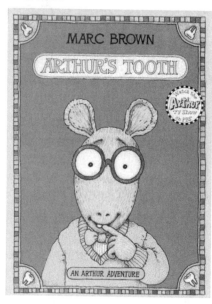

Cover from *Arthur's Nose* by Marc Brown © 1976. Cover from *Arthur's Tooth* by Marc Brown © 2005. Reprinted with permission from Little, Brown and Company.

doesn't look like the Arthur character I know. Here's the Arthur book I read the other day [hold up another Arthur book read aloud earlier, such as *Arthur's Tooth* (Brown, 2005; see Figure 18B)]. Even though the pictures of Arthur are different, I think I do have some knowledge because I already know the author, Marc Brown. I'm going to start reading to see if *Arthur's Nose* is part of the Arthur series.

During the read-aloud, the students discovered that *Arthur's Nose* was, in fact, part of the Arthur series because it had all the same characters they know from other Arthur books. As with any minilesson within reading workshop, students transitioned into independent reading time, sharing the prior knowledge they had about *Arthur's Nose*. On this day, students practiced *K*, knowledge prior to the book, as they made their own book selections or thought about *K* as it related to books currently in their book nooks.

Additional BOOKMATCH Lesson Starters

The following lesson starters can take place any time during the school year and do not necessarily have to serve as the first introductory minilesson of each of the BOOKMATCH criteria. Remember that your instruction of the criteria is ongoing. Readers need continual reinforcement of these concepts throughout the school year as they progress through the Phases of Learning. You will likely teach more than one minilesson on each criterion. Your students will guide these instructional decisions.

B—Book Length. Take a look at the book you've chosen for independent reading time today. Are you comfortable with the length of your book? Ask yourself, is this a good length for me?

O—Ordinary Language. I can see that you all have brought different books to the carpet today. Let's open our books to any page and read it aloud to a neighbor. Decide together if it sounds like talk and if you're comfortable with the way the book is written. Are you comfortable with the language of this book?

O—Organization. Today I want to talk about how a book is organized. Organization means a lot of different things. Talk to your neighbor about how your two books are different. Look at the pages, pictures, where the words are, special boxes, and the front and back cover. What are you noticing about the way your books are organized? I can see that Bailie's book has large pictures with some words on the page, but Christie's book has all words on the page....

K—Knowledge Prior to Book. Remember yesterday when we learned more about polar bears? I noticed that there is a polar bear on the front of this book. One of the things I want to do as a reader is to think about what I already know about polar bears. What are some of the things you remember learning about polar bears? All that information will help me when I start to read this book. Now look at the cover of your book....

M—Manageable Text. Before you go off to read today, I want you to think about the book you have in your hand right now and whether or not you can manage the text. What I mean is, you have to decide if the text or the words are too easy, too hard, or just right. Start reading your book from the beginning. How do you feel about the words? Do you understand what you read?

A—Appeal to Genre. We know that there are different types of books. Have you thought about what type of book you have right now? Look at our class genre chart. Where does your book fit on this chart? Have you read this genre before? Tell a reader next to you what you already know about this genre.

T—Topic Appropriateness. The other day, Macy chose a book about a dog that got lost. When she thought about the topic of the book it actually upset her, and she told me that she was not ready to read about the lost dog because her own dog is lost. I told her that was a very appropriate decision to make and that readers have to think about the topic of their books and whether or not they feel comfortable with the topic. It doesn't mean that Macy won't ever read this book, it just means that right now she is not comfortable.

C—Connection. As readers, we've been making so many connections to the books that are read to us. We've made text-to-text connections and text-to-self connections. Sometimes, we've even made connections to our world. Now let's talk about the connections we make to our own book choices. How can you relate to your book? Can you make a connection?

H—High-Interest. Readers, I called you together to learn from Danny. Danny has very specific interests. He likes basketball, Scooby Doo, and skateboarding. Because Danny knows what he likes, he can search for books that interest him. Yesterday he went to the sports container and chose a book on basketball, so he already knows that he is interested in this book. Alex also likes basketball and saw Danny choosing this book. So, Danny, you'll be able to give Alex your recommendation when you're done reading it.

Verbal Reinforcement During Minilessons

Keep in mind that with each new minilesson students gain even more understanding of self-selecting, which means you need to provide more time for them to practice. It helps to provide lots of verbal reinforcement as they're choosing a book. This kind of talk serves several purposes, such as praising appropriate behaviors, reminding readers of your expectations, and providing feedback. The following are some statements that we have used to encourage our students:

> I see someone looking at the pictures to see if they are interested. Courtney is probably thinking about whether she is interested in the topic of the book or what the book is about.

> I like how Macy is turning the pages of the book to think about the length. She even looked at the back cover for a summary.

> Paul is already quietly reading. Looks like he found a book match.

> Oh, isn't that interesting. Beth brought her book closer to the poster while she thinks about each question.

> Look how well you're doing, Jamal. You're remembering how important it is to use your book stick. Looks like you're interested in the science container. Let me know what you find.

By talking about the good behaviors you see, you are essentially influencing the behaviors of all students, because all students hear your words.

Abandoning: When a Book Doesn't Fit

You may notice that some of your readers put books back on the shelf before they finish reading them. This is called abandoning—the reader makes a decision to stop reading because the book just doesn't seem to fit. Abandoning is another example of a behavior that should be modeled and discussed for your capable and confident readers. Sometimes readers attribute abandoning to insufficient reading skills. However, we believe that helping readers understand why they might abandon books leads them to connect abandoning to a poor book match rather than to poor reading ability. Abandoning is something that all readers do, regardless of ability and attitude toward reading. We want students to understand that abandoning is natural and another part of the reading process. Having this knowledge creates readers who are more confident in their decision making. Of course, if you have a student who habitually abandons books, you will need to support this reader with conferences.

It is critical for your readers to learn how to explain their decision to abandon a book. The BOOKMATCH criteria provide the necessary language for students to clarify their thinking about and feelings toward a book. For example, after a minilesson on abandoning, first-grade students generated several reasons why they abandon books, and the teacher compiled these responses on a chart. The following are some of the reasons the class came up with for abandoning:

Because it was *too* long.

Maybe you get tired of the book because you've read it *so* many times already.

You know so much about it and what it is about.

Because you see another interesting book.

So you could learn some more from another book about the same topic.

The end might get sad and you don't want to read the sad part.

The function of abandoning is a critical lesson for parents to learn as well. We are reminded of a parent whose second-grade daughter selected a chapter book for her weekly reading log. After two days of reading the book, about halfway through the text, Christie told her mom that she didn't want to read the book anymore because she lost interest. Christie's mother questioned the classroom teacher and expressed concern that abandoning would become a pattern with her daughter. The teacher shared the criteria of BOOKMATCH to explain that readers sometimes lose interest if they don't make careful decisions about their book selections. Christie already knew that abandoning was an appropriate response and that several things may cause a reader to want to stop reading. Christie's mother realized that she didn't have choices about

PARENT CONNECTION

Depending on your school's calendar, you may choose to share BOOKMATCH at a Parent Night or Family Reading Night. We also use a Friday Folder system for ongoing parent communication. Parents are aware that anything in the Friday Folder is important information that requires their attention. In the Friday Folder, parents expect to read about the previous week's lessons, including BOOKMATCH experiences.

what she read when she was in school, and recalled several books she was forced to read that did not interest her. When she compared her experiences to Christie's, she no longer questioned the decision to abandon. She was, in fact, impressed by the sophisticated way in which Christie thought about books.

The teacher scheduled a reading conference later that day with Christie. She discovered that Christie lost interest because she was relying on a friend's recommendation and had not thought through other criteria before beginning the book. Christie wanted to exchange the book for one that offered more suspense and had more complex characters. The classroom teacher recommended several book series and sent Christie off to browse these titles with a BOOKMATCH form. Figure 19 shows Christie's selection process as she completed a student comment form (see the Appendix for reproducible versions of the student comment form). Christie's comments on the student form show that she has a very interesting connection to the book topic. She has some background

---

FIGURE 19
Christie's Student Comment Form for a New Book Found After Abandoning Original Selection

Criteria for Choosing Books	Student Comments
B Book Length Is this length too little, just right, or too much?	Just right
O Ordinary Language Does it make sense and sound like talk?	yes I can understand
O Organization How is the book structured?	pictures by the words chapters
K Knowledge Prior to Book What do I already know about this topic, this book, or this author?	I knew a littel about reptiles
M Manageable Text Are the words too easy, just right, or too hard?	Just right Sometimes hard word
A Appeal to Genre What is the genre and do I know this genre?	fiction
T Topic Appropriateness Am I comfortable with the topic of this book?	yes
C Connection Can I relate and make a connection to another book or real life experience?	a Snake almost sriked at me and my dad I was at the museum
H High-Interest Am I interested in finding out more?	when I first got the Book I was intrisrid in what hapind

knowledge and feels that the words provide the right amount of challenge for her. Christie ended up reading this text in its entirety and shortly thereafter became hooked on this new series.

The student comment form includes the selection criteria and space for the reader to record responses to the questions. Using the student comment forms allows you to capture each reader's self-selection thought process. Instructional uses of the form are presented in more detail in the next chapter along with several completed example forms.

Reflection Point

During independent reading time within your reading workshop, take field notes (what you see and hear). Using these notes as your guide, highlight what your readers are capable of regarding self-selection. Your field notes as well as the BOOKMATCH criteria can help you plan for future minilessons that will develop more confident readers.

CHAPTER 4

Moving Toward Independence: Confident Readers Become Autonomous

"I'm reading books I never thought I could read."
—A.J., first grader

In this chapter we discuss the shift in our instructional approach as students move through the confident phase to the autonomous phase in the pattern of implementing BOOKMATCH (see Figure 20). The teaching becomes more of a shared experience as students take on more responsibility for their learning. We will explain how shared demonstrations and BOOKMATCH interviews help students become more confident. Continued success in the confident phase eventually moves a learner to autonomy.

Building Readers' Confidence Toward Autonomy

At this point in the year, routines have been established for independent reading, the majority of the library has been sorted, and each letter of BOOKMATCH has been introduced and practiced. Remember, this consistent, daily practice with BOOKMATCH must continue through each Phase of Learning. In the confident Phase of Learning students are comfortable with their skills as independent readers. Students are able to reshelf books, use book sticks, choose new books with BOOKMATCH, and talk to a neighbor to confirm their book selections, as illustrated in Figure 21. And students are able to read—really read—and apply

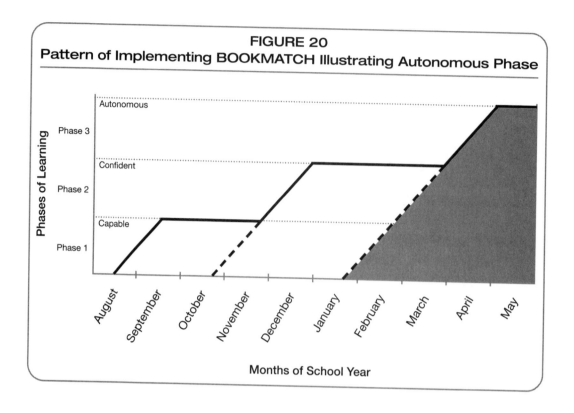

FIGURE 20
Pattern of Implementing BOOKMATCH Illustrating Autonomous Phase

strategies. In addition to self-selection strategies, comprehension and word attack strategies can be applied because students are reading just-right books that interest them. They're doing exactly what you taught them in minilessons and conferences, and they are continuing to take more responsibility for their own learning and the learning of others. With this responsibility comes the confidence and desire to participate in a way that is more public through shared demonstration and peer reviews.

Shared Demonstrations

A shared demonstration is when the teacher and a student or group of students share in the responsibility of teaching a minilesson for the other students in the classroom. In a shared demonstration, the teacher's role is one of facilitator, but there is still a very specific purpose to the lesson. A student is asked to become part of the instruction by sharing his or her own experiences as a learner. The other students are able to make authentic connections as learners themselves. A shared demonstration

Photograph by Dianna Dee Damkoehler. Used with permission.

resembles a think-aloud, because you and the student verbalize your thoughts as you make sense of something. Shared demonstrations provide the right amount of challenge and continue to build on readers' confidence. Shared demonstration lessons result in your careful observance of daily activity. Opportunities for powerful teaching moments reveal themselves when you browse students' book nooks, observe reading behaviors, take anecdotal notes, read student comment forms, and listen to your readers. These informal assessments guide instruction and help you locate students for shared demonstration lessons.

Shared Demonstrations of Student Comment Forms. The shared demonstration of student comment forms initiates a new phase of learning. At first you will fill out the students' comment forms during individual conferences so that reading time is not spent filling out the form. When students are ready, you can remove yourself from the process and hand that task over to the students. Readers often are eager to take on this responsibility.

As their teacher, you may sense that the students want and are ready for more responsibility. For example, when two students had the opportunity to fill out their own forms and share these with the rest of the class, it was clear we were moving into a new Phase of Learning. For a minilesson, Tuwanda and Paul demonstrated how they completed the student comment form as they made a book selection. The class saw Tuwanda's and Paul's forms in their own handwriting on the overhead. The reaction was powerful, as hands began to shoot in the air and multiple voices begged for the same opportunity. "Can I fill out my own form for my book match?" Any student who felt ready was allowed to fill out a form. Upon reading those completed forms, we realized that students had the understanding and were capable of taking over this task. At this point you should step back, because the scaffold is still there. Figure 22 provides examples of completed student comment forms from Macy, Paul, and Tuwanda. When you look across these three student comment forms, what you might notice is that all three students are revealing their thought processes at the time of self-selection. Both Tuwanda and Paul appear to understand each of the criteria of BOOKMATCH. Their understanding of the criteria was also confirmed during individual conferences with them. Their responses to the questions provide detailed and specific information, which is why they were asked to show their work to the rest of the class.

Macy's student comment form, however, shows limited thinking about the criteria. She is still learning and practicing matching herself to a just-right book. Some of her responses are repeated; it is clear that she needs more instruction about the organization of a book. Macy was pulled for a small group and an individual conference to talk about book

TIPS FOR INTERMEDIATE-GRADE READERS

You may want to have students in the intermediate grades fill out their own student comment forms from the start. You will want to have plenty of blank forms available as well as a system for managing and assessing these forms. Once the process of self-selection becomes automatic for a reader, you may choose to stop using the student comment form as a scaffold. Automaticity implies that the reader has internalized the criteria of BOOKMATCH.

FIGURE 22
Student Comment Forms Illustrating Varying Levels of Understanding of BOOKMATCH Criteria

A. Macy's Student Comment Form

Criteria for Choosing Books		Student Comments
B	**Book Length** Is this length too little, just right, or too much?	Just right
O	**Ordinary Language** Does it make sense and sound like talk?	yes
O	**Organization** How is the book structured?	(Text)
K	**Knowledge Prior to Book** What do I already know about this topic, this book, or this author?	I write to a Playadour it a
M	**Manageable Text** Are the words too easy, just right, or too hard?	Just right
A	**Appeal to Genre** What is the genre and do I know this genre?	funny Book
T	**Topic Appropriateness** Am I comfortable with the topic of this book?	yes
C	**Connection** Can I relate and make a connection to another book or real life experience?	I write too a Playadout it a
H	**High-Interest** Am I interested in finding out more?	yes

B. Paul's Student Comment Form

Criteria for Choosing Books		Student Comments
B	**Book Length** Is this length too little, just right, or too much?	Just right.
O	**Ordinary Language** Does it make sense and sound like talk?	Yes.
O	**Organization** How is the book structured?	Lots of pictures. But Not on every page.
K	**Knowledge Prior to Book** What do I already know about this topic, this book, or this author?	the atnor make a series of It.
M	**Manageable Text** Are the words too easy, just right, or too hard?	Just right.
A	**Appeal to Genre** What is the genre and do I know this genre?	I know It. chapter book.
T	**Topic Appropriateness** Am I comfortable with the topic of this book?	Yes.
C	**Connection** Can I relate and make a connection to another book or real life experience?	getting lost in my video game.
H	**High-Interest** Am I interested in finding out more?	Yes.

C. Tuwanda's Student Comment Form

Criteria for Choosing Books		Student Comments
B	**Book Length** Is this length too little, just right, or too much?	It's probably a little bit long but I think I can do it.
O	**Ordinary Language** Does it make sense and sound like talk?	yes.
O	**Organization** How is the book structured?	not vary meny pitchers. And where there is they are not in the pitcher.
K	**Knowledge Prior to Book** What do I already know about this topic, this book, or this author?	I'v ben reading the seres.
M	**Manageable Text** Are the words too easy, just right, or too hard?	thar are a few words I had to yos stradages on.
A	**Appeal to Genre** What is the genre and do I know this genre?	It is fantasy.
T	**Topic Appropriateness** Am I comfortable with the topic of this book?	yes.
C	**Connection** Can I relate and make a connection to another book or real life experience?	I'v read other Magic tree house books
H	**High-Interest** Am I interested in finding out more?	rely.

structure. This phase of students' filling out their own forms resumes the upward slope of implementation that moves readers toward autonomy.

Another example of shared demonstration involves the participation of the whole group. We started to notice that students had limited responses on the student comment form for *O*—organization. Perhaps this happened because organization is a broad concept and there are so many different ways that books are structured. In addition, several of our students individually asked for clarification about organization, so we made the decision to hold a whole-group sharing session. Figure 23 shows the product of one class's brainstorming possibilities. This became a reference chart that students could use to help them when they were thinking about organization. Before beginning the brainstorming, students were asked to grab several books from the "Books to Be Returned" container and meet at the carpet. The following discussion by the teacher illustrates this shared demonstration:

> I'm glad you're ready with books in your hands because we need to use those to teach one another about O—organization. The organization of a book is the structure of the book. Structure means where things are in your book or what things are in your book. For example, where are

FIGURE 23
Student Using the Brainstorming Organization Chart

Photograph by Dianna Dee Damkoehler. Used with permission.

the pictures? Where are the words? Are there any special boxes or sections? How is your book laid out differently from other books? What's on the front, what's on the back? Let's teach one another all about organization by sharing all these different structures of books. I'll write your ideas about organization and structure on this chart as you share them with all of us.

The chart in Figure 23 reveals that the students are now more aware of the many features within texts, such as section titles, illustrations, page numbers, borders, summaries, speech bubbles, captions, and labels.

Shared Demonstrations of BOOKMATCH Criteria. Another opportunity for shared demonstration may present itself while looking through students' book nooks. You'll know enough about your readers at this point in the year that you can easily and quickly browse their book nooks for appropriate choices about once per week. This is not a time for a teacher to control the selection process by removing books, but to observe how the selection process is going for individuals. For example, Isaiah had a text in his book nook that was obviously too difficult for him. He was focusing on his interest in hurricanes, but ignoring all the other criteria for book selection. Therefore, rather than just tell him the book was too difficult, we wanted him to figure it out for himself. This minilesson was used as a learning opportunity for the whole group. Even though students have already had some instruction and practice with M—manageable text, you'll find that reinforcement is necessary throughout the year.

Isaiah was asked to justify his book selection in a shared demonstration to provide some reinforcement, as illustrated in the discussion that follows:

Teacher: Today we are going to learn from one of our classmates. We are all teachers in here. Isaiah has agreed to help us by talking about one of the books in his book nook. Isaiah, I notice that you have this very long book all about hurricanes. Could you hold up that book? Turn to a few pages so the class can see what the text and pictures look like. Wow, you have really challenged yourself as a reader. What did you think about as a reader when you chose this book?

Isaiah: Well, I really like hurricanes. I saw a show about them with my dad. The pictures look real.

Teacher: Great, you definitely have high interest with hurricanes, and you chose a topic that you are comfortable with. In the show you watched, you probably learned some information about hurricanes.

Isaiah: Yeah, they can destroy a home or even like our whole town.

Teacher: So, you have knowledge prior to the book. I wonder, Isaiah, can you show us what you did when you thought about *B—book length*?

Isaiah: I didn't really do that.

Teacher: Good readers will think about more than just the topic and what interests them. So, Isaiah, check the book length now, so you can show everybody that you know how to. Notice how Isaiah is opening up the book, looking at the pages...Isaiah, what do you think? How does this book fit you for *B—book length*?

Isaiah: Well, it's kinda long. I mostly just looked at the pictures.

Teacher: Then, we'd better look at the text because you need to be a reader. Do you remember when we talked about *M—manageable text*? Go ahead, Isaiah, you know what to do. Turn to any page and start reading out loud. Only this time, when you come to a word you can't get even after using your strategies, hold up a finger. [teacher demonstrates by holding one finger in the air]

CLARIFICATION SPOT

The five-finger rule is a widely known strategy for students to determine text difficulty, and it complements the instruction of *M—manageable text*.

At this point Isaiah reads aloud and students listen and watch. He ends up with five fingers in the air before finishing a page. Isaiah has discovered that this text is too difficult and at the same time demonstrated the use of the five-finger rule:

Teacher: Okay, stop there. You're holding up five fingers. You're telling me that you already had five hard words on one page. Isaiah, you really helped us because I'm going to explain the five-finger rule. When you choose a book, you must think about *M*—manageable text. This is how hard the words are for you as a reader. One way you can do that is to use the five-finger rule, just like Isaiah did. Each time you come to a word that is too hard, you hold up one finger. A word that is too hard is a word that you've already tried to read and attack, but you just can't get it, and it doesn't seem to make sense. If you get to five fingers on one page, that book is too hard. Isaiah, is this book too hard, too easy, or just right?

Isaiah: Too hard.

Teacher: I think you are right. This book on hurricanes is too hard. I like how you figured that out. [to whole class] Today while you're reading, I'll be watching. I'll be looking for fingers in the air. So, if you come to a word you don't know and using your strategies doesn't work, put your finger up. Each time you have to do this, hold up another finger. That way, without having to even come to you, I can see how you're doing with that book. Before you go off to read, let's remember the two things that Isaiah taught us. First, good readers have to think about more than just what they're interested in when choosing a just-right book. Second, we can use the five-finger rule to decide if the words in the book are too hard. [A transition begins here.]

As the teacher, if you see a student with five fingers in the air, you can immediately provide assistance. It is a good idea to look for patterns as well. If one or two students always have lots of fingers in the air, you may want to pull out those students for a guided group.

We think shared demonstrations are powerful teaching experiences that immediately affect the learning environment. Our informal daily assessments guide our decisions about what type of shared demonstration is best to maintain engagement throughout the Phases of Learning. Goodman (1996) confirms that when students "are in environments where what they have to say about their reading and the reading of others is taken seriously, the language that is necessary to discuss the issues emerges" (p. 608).

BOOKMATCH Interviews

In a BOOKMATCH interview the students lead the class in an explanation of book choices as others ask questions. An interview is an unscripted discussion during the course of the sharing. It can involve the teacher and the students, or just the students. While the shared demonstration lessons allow the teacher to prepare ahead of time based on an instructional need or purpose, an interview unfolds naturally in the moment.

As students move through Phase 2 of the learning, they have the confidence to explain their ability to choose just-right books in an interview. In a reciprocal environment, students expect a chance to share their success. We have students put a sticky note with their name on the cover of their book match and place the book on the teacher's desk. Students know that this is a way for them to get on the agenda for a future reading workshop minilesson.

Table 7 illustrates an example of a daily schedule. Notice that the BOOKMATCH interview is a priority, and is important enough to be written on the board as part of the daily schedule. Sometimes several students want to share, so it may take a few days to interview them all. But they all know they will get a chance. You may have a different way of managing how students will sign up for a BOOKMATCH interview. While we have students place a book on the teacher's desk, you may prefer to

---

TABLE 7
Sample Daily Schedule for Classrooms
With Readers at Confident Stage

Big Book = strategies

BOOKMATCH interview = Tim

Independent reading
    (small group)
      (conferences = John, Suzanne)

Writing workshop—poetry

PE/lunch/recess

Math—inches

Library

Social studies—maps

use a container in the classroom or even a sign-up sheet. What matters is that you have the time to preview the book selection before the interview.

When it's time for the interview we put a stool in the front of the room, making this moment special and important. Let students know it's time for a BOOKMATCH interview. Ask the interviewee to get his or her just-right book, while you get the BOOKMATCH questions. We think it is important to bring out the BOOKMATCH poster during the interview, because you may still be scaffolding several readers through the book selection questions. The poster provides a visual reference for the kinds of questions that students can ask.

We let the students decide on the structure of their interviews. They can choose to let other students ask questions first, or they can begin with their explanation of why they have a book match. Sometimes this begins with readers talking about their student comment forms. The interview includes questions from the audience about why the book is right for the reader.

The audience members always surprise us during the interview. As the teacher, you should just sit back and be amazed. Students may ask a question directly from the poster or they may be so comfortable with the language that they use their own words to ask the questions. The following examples illustrate what we've heard our own students ask:

What did you think about the length?

Did you end up making a connection?

Were you able to read it?

What did you think about the topic?

Did you know anything ahead of time?

This kidwatching (Goodman, 1985) experience provides a great opportunity for anecdotal notes. The interview conversations will reveal strengths and weaknesses of readers regarding self-selection. You will want to use this data to plan for your future minilessons and guided groups.

The following dialogue demonstrates an early experience with the BOOKMATCH interview. You'll notice that the teacher is modeling for the audience how to ask questions and conduct an interview. For this experience, the teacher sits on the carpet as another interviewer.

Teacher:	It's time for a BOOKMATCH interview. I'd like you to turn your eyes and bodies and make sure you are sitting in a way that you can see. Turn your eyes toward Joe and Emma. Joe and Emma put notes on their books, letting me know they had a book match. Emma has a book called *Talk, Talk, Talk* [Cowley, 1997]. Joe's book is called *The Best Book of Big Cats* [Gunzi, 2001]. I'm going to get the poster out so you can be reminded of some of the questions you might ask during this interview. Emma and Joe, how would you like to do the interview today? Do you want to just start sharing, or do you want us to ask you questions? [both Joe and Emma have agreed to just have questions] Okay, let's start asking our questions. I'll go first. What's your connection to *Talk, Talk, Talk*?
Emma:	Sometimes I talk to my brother a lot.
Brock:	Um, Is the length just right, too little, or too much?
Emma and Joe:	Just right!
Brock:	That looks...for you...too long, Joe.
Joe:	Nuh uh. [looking at the teacher for support]
Teacher:	Actually, Joe has grown quite a bit as a reader and now that's a good length for Joe, I agree with him.
Joe:	I can read a page for you.
Teacher:	That's a great idea, because then we can ask you about *M*.

Joe reads a page out loud. It is determined that his text is a good match regarding difficulty. Emma then asks to read a page, and it is clear that the text is too easy, as illustrated in the dialogue that follows:

Teacher:	What about you, Emma, do you think your book is too hard, just right, or too easy?
Emma:	Just right.
Laine:	I think it's too E-A-S-Y. [spells out the word]
Teacher:	Laine thinks it's too easy. Does anyone else think that?

All students:	Yeah!!!!!
Joe:	I've read that book before.
Teacher:	For Emma, she needs to think about challenging herself more as a reader with the length and the words in the book.
Jamal:	She could abandon that book and get a new one.
Paul:	How is the book structured?
Joe:	In my book the pictures are all over with a little bit of words.
Emma:	The pictures are in boxes and the words are underneath. [Emma holds the book open so students can see what she means]
Anna:	What is the genre of the book and do you know this genre?
Joe:	I have a learning book.
Emma:	I have a learning book, too.
Nick:	In Joe's book it's information, so nonfiction but Emma's book is just a story book.
Teacher:	So, Emma's would be fiction and Joe's would be nonfiction?
Leah:	No, Emma's is a picture book. [more discussion follows about fiction and nonfiction and the terms *story book* and *picture book*]

After you have modeled the process of interviewing, you will need to step back and allow the students to take ownership of the interviews. Let students know how impressed you are with the way they have taken responsibility for their own learning and recognized the differences in other learners. These interviews are one example of how we create a community of learners who sincerely care about the learning of everyone. This is when you know it is time to sit back and watch them.

In the following dialogue, you will notice that the teacher's role has become that of an observer, allowing students to carry the conversation in the interview. It will probably be hard for you not to talk now that students have control of the process; however, we suggest that you be patient and give the students plenty of wait time. We found that it was easier to pull back when we made it clear to students that we just wanted to take notes while they talked. You'll find that it will be well worth it. Shauntae decided to begin her interview by sharing her book selection process before taking questions.

Shauntae: I'm going to start by sharing my form. Well, the book length was just right. It sounded like talk. For organization it had speech bubbles...like two on each page. I know a lot about camping because I've read about camping before. I read a lot of camping books like an American Girl Doll book. I was interested in finding out more.

Marcus: How does the American Girl Doll book go with it?

Shauntae: It was about camping.

Alysse: Have you ever been camping?

Shauntae: No, just read a lot of books about it.

Macy: When you first picked up the book, were you interested in the topic because the title said hiking and camping?

Shauntae: Yes.

Brock: Have you ever been hiking before?

Shauntae: Yep.

Christie: What's the number one reason that it was a book match?

Shauntae: It was mostly because of the connection.

Brock: Do you have any...I forgot, oh wait...do you have any hiking or camping books at home?

Shauntae: Yes.

Each of the interview examples shows how students have acquired the language of BOOKMATCH. We believe that these interviews are evidence of students' thinking critically about book selection and their own reading processes. These students, after all, are in first grade, yet have successfully acquired this sophisticated language and skill in critical thinking. We think it's important that all the readers in the classroom have an opportunity to be the focus of a minilesson involving some aspect of BOOKMATCH, whether it be by participating in an interview, sharing a student comment form, or providing a teaching moment from which others may learn. These experiences provide the foundation for the upward movement toward Phase 3: Autonomy.

How to Know When Students Are Ready for Autonomy

By about six months into the school year, students have had plenty of guided practice as they move through the Phases of Learning toward autonomy. In the pattern of implementing BOOKMATCH (see Figure 20 on page 60), you'll notice that the plateau at the end of Phase 2 extends for a longer period of time. This happens because students need time to practice and fine-tune what you've been teaching them. Explicit instruction about BOOKMATCH is gradually decreased, although students use BOOKMATCH each time they select a new book. They realize that they have a slightly different experience with each new book they consider. At the same time they are becoming better readers in terms of ability, which also affects the books they're browsing (see Figure 24). In this photo you can see that Melanie is engaged in her selection of a just-right book, while Aggie is carefully browsing through the new books container. Students look at new genres and new topics that maybe they did not try at the beginning of the year. They are reaching personal goals. This means that you will need to continue bringing new books into the library and students will continue to sort these new books.

When a reader reaches the autonomous phase, it means that he or she has internalized the book-selection criteria of BOOKMATCH. In the autonomous phase, a reader's self-selection of just-right books is

FIGURE 24
Students Browsing and Engaged in Independent Reading

Photograph by Dianna Dee Damkoehler. Used with permission

automatic, and the reader is aware of his or her reading identity. The reader uses the language of BOOKMATCH to discuss books and teach others how to self-select just-right books. At this point, students should be leading the instruction by what they say and do. They make the suggestions for minilessons because they have become experts in decision making to maintain the appropriate flow of activity. The dialogue in your classroom environment is primarily in the voices of your readers. You should hear students engaging in book talk about various topics, including the following:

- recommendations
- character development
- authors
- reading strategies

- illustrations
- interesting facts from nonfiction
- preferences
- series
- reading/writing connections

Once you know that students have been in the plateau of Phase 2 for a while and are ready to move to autonomy (see Figure 20 on page 60), provide them with opportunities to teach others about BOOKMATCH to strengthen their understanding. For example, you may have your students teach book buddies from upper grades how to use BOOKMATCH. You could also have students teach their parents or volunteers who visit the classroom. And, of course, you'll want them to teach the principal of your school. If they're successful in this teaching, we know that they will leave us armed with a tool for self-selection that will become part of what they do inherently as readers in later years. When our students were asked, "What is BOOKMATCH?" at the beginning of May, their responses indicated that BOOKMATCH had become a part of their identities as readers who are capable of self-selecting just-right books. The following student responses to that question illustrate this autonomy:

Brian: It's thinking about a book that's just right for you.

Jamal: Different letters and questions that you ask to yourself. If you do all of them and say yes, then you have a book match.

Sammie: If you have a book, ask yourself the questions, and you really read it all and you like it.

Nicole: If you have a connection to it and it's the right book for you. You just gotta check off every part of BOOKMATCH and then you'll probably know.

Of course, every classroom of students will be different in terms of their reading ability, background knowledge, support from home, and the degree to which they are immersed in literacy. For some students, autonomy may not emerge right away, or even during one school year. All students will need ongoing instruction regarding strategies and comprehension as texts become more difficult and complex. As they transition to the upper grades, all students face new challenges; however, we have instilled a passion for free voluntary reading. Inevitably your class moves on to the next teacher, so each future teacher must sustain this passion and continue building students' confidence. Having this strong foundation allows readers to take ownership of their learning.

We take pride in knowing that we have prepared our students with the tools and skills to be autonomous literacy learners—literacy learners who do not have to rely on others to make decisions. We have no doubt that our students know how to choose just-right books. Isaiah will think about more than just what interests him, Emma will make selections that challenge her as a reader, and Shauntae is equipped with the language necessary to explain her choices.

Reflection Point

Observe your students talking with other students about the books from their book nooks. How do you see the language of autonomy and BOOKMATCH occurring in those authentic conversations? What does this mean for your instruction?

(**CHAPTER 5**)

Managing the Data:
Accountability
and Conferences
With BOOKMATCH

"While the emphasis in reading conferences was always on sharing rather than testing, these conferences did provide me with an invaluable source of data for anecdotal evaluative records on aspects of a child's total language development."
—Jan D'Arcy, "Talking in the Reading Conference," in J. Dwyer's *A Sea of Talk*

There is no doubt that the independent reading component of your reading workshop is full of possibilities for meaningful learning. Managing those possibilities involves a structured approach, commitment, and the belief that students are capable and responsible learners. Management is a process contingent on the establishment of routines and consistent expectations. With a workshop approach you can create a well-maintained and functioning environment where students know that they are held accountable.

This chapter will address manageability and accountability. Holding your students and yourself accountable during the independent reading time of your reading workshop involves a clear management system. We will present several management techniques that work for us, but you will likely need to customize these options. At the very least, your management system will need to produce data that gives you immediate feedback about your readers' learning. We will show this data collection through reading conferences. Don't forget about the importance and value of careful, daily observation to support the other tangible data collected:

Learning from careful observation is basic to all scientific endeavors; learning from our students as we watch them learn is important not only for the planning of curriculum and instruction but also for constantly expanding our knowledge about teaching and learning. (Goodman, 1996, p. 600)

Knowing this, we will discuss how to use running records, student comment forms, anecdotal notes, and retellings within reading conferences to assess how well students choose books that are just right for them. Each day, while your students self-select books, hold discussions, and participate as readers, you should collect evidence of student growth. You will be able to use all of this information to report to parents, colleagues, and administrators.

Reading Conferences

A reading conference is invaluable time spent one-on-one with a reader. Any time you talk one-on-one with a reader about a book, you are conducting a conference. Reading conferences should be brief, purposeful, and individualized. Some teachers may have a system in place for meeting with students on a weekly basis; others may meet with students more informally on an as-needed basis. Either way, reading conferences begin with a clear purpose and may be initiated by the student or the teacher. Think of it as a "checking in" time. The reading conference allows you to provide attention to one reader at a time. Your goal should be to meet with every student at least once per week in a conference. Of course, things come up—Monday holidays, Wednesday field trips, and Friday assemblies. However, just asking "How's it going today?" begins a conversation with each reader and shows readers that they are being held accountable. Your presence, sliding up a chair next to theirs, reminds them of the expectations for reading time. And when done consistently and well, they all want to meet with you every day to show you what they can do. No two conferences will be the same. Some may be very brief—a couple of minutes—and others may take up to 10 minutes. The length of the conference depends on the purpose, the student, and the text involved.

Purposeful conferences are an essential component for independent reading. In conferences we're always checking to make sure that students are reading just-right books. Routman (2003) explains,

It is our job as knowledgeable professionals to ensure that our students are reading when [and what] they are supposed to be reading; that means that they are effectively using phonics, word analysis, comprehension strategies, and whatever else they bring to the text to understand it. Otherwise, we are squandering precious time. (p. 104)

Conferences should occur for the self-selected books and not for a leveled book received during a guided group. Before you sit down with a reader, you should take a few moments to "call up" your own knowledge of this reader. What is the student currently reading? What did you talk about in the last conference? What are his or her current interests? Use your knowledge to individualize the conference and build on the data you already have about each reader.

Conference Management

You probably won't begin a system of reading conferences until you and your readers are comfortable with the routine of independent reading. This may take a month or two. This doesn't mean, however, that you won't be having brief conversations with individual students from the start. Early conversations won't be as structured regarding a purpose, but rather will praise appropriate behaviors and redirect inappropriate ones. Such consistent praise and redirection sets the foundation for an ideal learning environment that allows for individual conferences.

As soon as you realize that students are self-sufficient, self-selecting, and engaged in independent reading you can begin to implement reading conferences, although you will continue to praise and redirect behaviors throughout the school year. We prepare our students for conferences by first explaining what a reading conference is. We model them in whole-group instruction by holding a mock conference with a selected reader to show students what they might expect and experience. This minilesson is brief and provides an opportunity to remind students that their routine doesn't change, and neither does their role as a reader. The conference only changes the teacher's role during independent reading time. The early conferences will be driven by the teacher, but your readers will gradually take more of the responsibility (D'Arcy, 1989).

We usually begin implementing conferences by randomly choosing students. The

CLARIFICATION SPOT

During your modeling of reading conferences to your students, you should remind them that they should not interrupt when you're conferring with other students; rather they are asked to be smart thinkers, rely on others for help, or wait until the conference is over. Follow through with the consequences of whatever your schoolwide behavior plan might be to promote good choices.

purpose of the random selection is to establish the routine of conferring. Students need time to observe the process and become comfortable with continuing their reading despite this "intrusion." For the first several weeks, move around the room often. This way, students can get used to the movement and it will become natural.

Conferences can take place anywhere. You may prefer to have a designated spot in the classroom where students come to you. You could pull up a chair next to a student at his or her desk or table spot. Students love when you join them on the floor or in their favorite corner.

Proximity and exposure are hidden benefits of conducting a reading conference at a student's table spot. For example, when Jessica (second author) pulls up a chair next to Bailie at her table, Owen, Brock, and Mikayla get drawn into the instruction as well. They watch, they listen, but eventually, they turn back to their own reading, armed with new knowledge.

You will keep track of which students you've visited, the dates, purposes of the conferences, and other anecdotal notes. We use a conference binder to keep track of time spent with individual students. This binder contains a tab for each student that includes notebook paper, student comment forms, and reading logs (see the Appendix for reproducible student comment forms and reading logs).

You may feel overwhelmed at the thought of conferring with all of your students. However, it is possible if you keep the following suggestions in mind:

- You don't need to see everyone the same number of times. For example, you may have seen Aubrey on Monday but need to see her again on Tuesday based on what happened on Monday.

- You don't want to overlook someone. For example, Adrianna is pulled out for special services each day, but you'll still need to touch base with her.

- You don't need to confer with the same students you just had in a guided group. Immediate needs for these students would be addressed during the group time.

The following are other management possibilities for making sure all your readers receive individual attention:

- Assign a day for each reader; however, keep in mind that needs of the students vary from day to day, week to week, or book to book.

- Designate a location for listing the names of students who will have conferences that day.

- Keep a copy of your class list taped to the front of a conference binder. Write the date you visit next to the student's name. This gives you a quick visual of who's been seen and who is overdue. Even the brief, "How's it going?" conferences are recorded on this sheet.

- Visit all students at one table each day.

- Hang a sign-up sheet for students to request conferences.

Situations That Call for Conferences

While one student's conference might be about decoding and strategies, another student's conference might be on the selection process or direct teaching of BOOKMATCH criteria. Following are some different reasons for conducting a reading conference, using as examples reading conference scenarios from our own classrooms.

A student's book nook is filled—or overfilled—with inappropriate books. The teacher becomes aware that Tuwanda's book nook is jam-packed with self-selected books. Tuwanda is asked to gather the books from her book nook and meet the teacher at the reading table. Together they sort through and return books as necessary.

A student requests a conference. The teacher finds a note on her desk from Daniel requesting a conference for the following day. Daniel becomes the priority for a conference. He shares his excitement about being able to read a chapter book he chose on his own.

A student would benefit from an individual lesson to reinforce comprehension strategies. Several days after whole-group instruction on understanding a story's theme (author's message), the teacher realizes that Tamyra could use additional support. The same lesson is repeated one-on-one, just for Tamyra, using her book of choice.

A student's management of the text needs to be monitored. The teacher conducts a running record on Clair by asking where she is in her

CLARIFICATION SPOT

A reading folder is a two-pocket folder that holds artifacts of independent reading time, such as reading logs and student comment forms. We usually begin using reading folders in the second half of the year. Students have their own folder that they store in their book nook or at their table spot. We recommend using solid color folders for students to decorate, label, and personalize.

book and beginning the assessment there. This running record becomes part of Clair's reading folder after the teacher shares what she noticed about Clair as a reader.

A student would benefit from additional instruction on reading strategies used specifically for attacking words. One of Evette's reading goals is to use more than one strategy for unknown words. The teacher conducts a running record to see whether Evette is making progress. Additional instruction occurs about chunking words. The teacher connects this lesson to *M*—manageable text on the BOOKMATCH form so that Evette will continue to use this strategy when she comes to something she doesn't know in her self-selections.

A student would benefit from a one-on-one discussion about using BOOKMATCH for selecting a just-right book. The teacher brings a student comment form to a conference with Jorge. Together, they talk through the criteria as Jorge makes decisions about whether the book is just right for him.

A student needs a reminder of reading workshop expectations. During independent reading time, Mauricio becomes distracted by his new watch and wants to show all the students around him. The teacher sees this behavior and announces, "Mauricio, you're up next for a conference." In the brief conference, Mauricio receives a verbal warning and is respectfully reminded of the expectation that he be a reader during independent reading time. Mauricio is well aware of the consequences if he does not redirect himself.

The teacher would like the opportunity to ask a student, "How's it going?" Mikayla is independent in all areas. The teacher makes a point of checking in with her, even if just to ask how she's doing. The teacher verifies that Mikayla continues to gain meaning from more challenging texts and that the content is appropriate. Mikayla continues to use BOOKMATCH successfully to choose new books.

A student was engaged in one of his or her book choices and would benefit from a discussion of literature for pure enjoyment. Joe has just finished his first Ricky Ricotta's Mighty Robot book by Dav Pilkey. He can't stop talking about all the silly parts. The teacher shares the parts she thinks are funny, too, and recommends other books in that series. Joe recommends the book to his friends after the conference.

Responding to Students During a Reading Conference

Your role in a conference depends on the purpose of the conference. At any given time, you may find yourself being a listener, note taker, teacher, coach, cheerleader, or learner. The way you respond will depend on the role you take. We like to start the conferences by asking a general question, such as "What are you reading?" or "How are you doing as a reader today?" The first step is to listen and learn. You may ask the same question to every reader with whom you confer, but you will get different responses because they are all reading different books and have differing reading strengths and weaknesses. In other words, you may be prepared to have the conference, but you can't always be prepared for the way the reader will respond, or for his or her needs at that time. That's why you need to be comfortable taking on a variety of roles in the conference. This is often your time to respond as one reader to another without prescribed answers, as illustrated in the following example.

One day in class Colby approached his teacher with flushed cheeks and shyly asked if he can meet with her to show her his book. He was proud that he had chosen this book on his own and that he could read it. The teacher asked Colby if he wanted to have a conference the next day. Because this was a student-requested conference, the teacher prepared herself to be a listener and a note taker.

The teacher also considered what she knew about Colby. Both of Colby's sisters were very strong readers at his age, while Colby excelled in math. He was motivated and would choose to read a book before morning assembly while most students chose to play around and talk with friends. He received speech support twice a week and often missed out on conference time. Colby lacked confidence as a reader, but he worked very hard with the goal in mind of being able to read a chapter book. The teacher knew that she might need to be a cheerleader for Colby as he continued to build his confidence. The conference began like any other with a general question to get Colby talking.

Teacher: What's going well for you?

Colby: I made a book match.

Teacher: That's great! Tell me how you know. I'm going to write this down so we can tell other readers about it.

FIGURE 25
Teacher-Completed Student Comment Form and Running Record

A. Colby's Teacher-Completed Student Comment Form Based on Conference

B. Teacher's Running Record for Colby

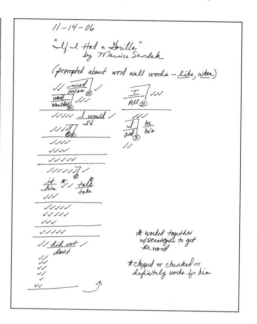

Criteria for Choosing Books		Student Comments
B	**Book Length** Is this length too little, just right, or too much?	"It's just perfect."
O	**Ordinary Language** Does it make sense and sound like talk?	"Yeah, I did."
O	**Organization** How is the book structured?	"Pictures + words."
K	**Knowledge Prior to Book** What do I already know about this topic, this book, or this author?	"Nothing."
M	**Manageable Text** Are the words too easy, just right, or too hard?	"Just right."
A	**Appeal to Genre** What is the genre and do I know this genre?	"Fiction."
T	**Topic Appropriateness** Am I comfortable with the topic of this book?	"Oh yeah, I really like animals."
C	**Connection** Can I relate and make a connection to another book or real life experience?	"I saw a gorilla in my life. I think that's it."
H	**High-Interest** Am I interested in finding out more?	"Yes—something about the gorilla w/ the boy."

Colby's student comment form—completed by the teacher during this conference—is provided in Figure 25. Filling out the form for Colby while having a conversation models the process of thinking through the criteria while choosing a book (see Figure 25A). The teacher also took a running record to see how he did (see Figure 25B). Using her knowledge that Colby lacked confidence, the teacher praised him for using the chop method, a chunking reading strategy. She shared with Colby that he should continue to use the chunking strategy because it works well for him when he comes to hard or unknown words. She also pointed out places where he self-corrected and fixed words on his own. She agreed with Colby that he did make a book match.

The teacher also used the opportunity to spotlight Colby's achievement during that day's whole-group wrap up.

Documents from Brian's conference tell us that he has selected a book that is too difficult and not a good match. When cross referencing the data, we could see that there were inconsistencies among the student comment form, the running record, and the retelling. This running record is taken from the beginning of page 2 of *Racing Stripes* by David Schmidt (2005). Brian was not using his strategies effectively. For most of the unknown words, Brian appealed to the teacher for help. His body language clearly indicated that he was becoming frustrated, so the teacher decided to stop the reading. Brian was not able to retell what he had just read. The teacher reminded Brian of the five-finger rule previously taught in a whole-group minilesson and of the criteria and questions on BOOKMATCH.

In order to support Brian's needs, the teacher went back to just two criteria on the student comment form and asked Brian to focus on *B* and *M* for his next selection. During the conference, Brian is sent off to find a just-right book from the "new books" container using *B* and *M*. The teacher needed to verify that Brian could be successful with just this much of BOOKMATCH before she ended the conference. When Brian brought back his selection to the teacher, she took a second running record to confirm his book choice. The teacher ended the conference and made a note to meet with Brian the next day to check his comprehension of this new selection. The teacher's goal will be to meet with Brian on a consistent basis to gradually reteach the other letters of BOOKMATCH.

Just like other paperwork you gather from students, student comment forms and running records should be revisited and used to plan for future instruction, whether it's in whole-group, small-group, or one-on-one settings. We like to fit in time to review all documentation from the day's conferences that same day. This could happen during a planning time, lunch time, or after school. Eventually, this paperwork gets filed in a conference binder, reading folder, or other system you have created.

Reading folders are useful for managing some of the data collected and for holding students accountable. These folders typically contain student work such as reading logs and student comment forms (once students start filling out their own forms). We use the reading folders when students are in the confident Phase of Learning. With confidence comes more responsibility. We expect students to maintain these folders and bring them to conferences. At any given time, we could look inside the folders to see recently read books and brief responses to these books. We usually collected the reading folders about once every two weeks to

browse for evidence of engagement and potential needs for conferences. Completed reading logs tell us what books were read over a period of time; whether the reader committed to a book; preferences for genres, authors, and topics; comprehension levels; and metacognitive awareness of strategies used while reading.

Data collected from reading conferences, reading logs, and observations can be compiled to show accountability of instructional outcomes for administrators or state and district mandates. Rubrics are a way to organize all of your knowledge and your students' hard work by reporting individual performance as compared to expectations. Rubrics are written in a clear and concise way so that they are reader friendly to parents and administrators. The structure of rubrics helps support differentiated instruction because they tell you what a student knows and still needs to learn. We like to design and use rubrics that characterize students' strengths and weaknesses as they relate to our instruction (Stanford & Siders, 2001). Rather than share these specific rubrics with students, we use them to record a student's progress toward the instructional goals. Therefore, our rubrics provide space for our comments within each goal.

The Appendix includes two reproducible rubrics that we have used successfully with primary-age students, which could be easily adapted for older readers or your classroom structure. These rubrics allow for both

quantitative and qualitative data. The quantitative data comes from the point values you designate to correspond with criteria or performance indicators. The qualitative data can be recorded in the boxes next to each performance indicator. You may want to adapt these to fit the needs of your students and your assessments.

We believe that rubrics for reading workshop are better used as a way to monitor our teaching. When you sit down to write a rubric, you really have to think about what you want students to know and the degree to which they may learn. Well-designed rubrics help us to "clarify our learning goals, design instruction that addresses those goals, communicate the goals to students, guide our feedback on students' progress toward the goals, and judge final products in terms of the degree to which the goals were met" (Andrade, 2005, p. 27).

Reflection Point

Conduct several reading conferences for a variety of purposes. In what roles did you find yourself—listener, note taker, teacher, coach, cheerleader, or learner? In what ways did the purpose of the conference change your role(s)?

CHAPTER 6

Measures of Success: Portraits of BOOKMATCH Readers

"One of the most important ways you will become more effective at teaching reading is through responding to your students' needs."
—Susan Davis Lenski & Susan L. Nierstheimer, *Becoming a Teacher of Reading: A Developmental Approach*

In this chapter we present portraits of three readers from our first-grade classrooms and their experiences with BOOKMATCH. The profiles of these three students—Ronnie, Aggie, and Corey—provide a glimpse into the different reading behaviors that you may see in your own classroom throughout your implementation of BOOKMATCH and independent reading. Rather than label a reader as low, average, or high, we like to describe typical reading behaviors of developing readers. We look at our readers in terms of development. Each reader comes to us with different experiences regarding books and self-selection. Their reading behaviors are a direct result of their prior experiences. These reading behaviors are valued in a way that allows them to progress at their own developmental pace.

We have identified three different levels of progress in students' increasing success with self-selection behaviors: reluctant, transitional, and self-directed (Wedwick & Wutz, 2006). Reluctant, transitional, and self-directed behaviors are one way to characterize how readers perform regarding self-selection in a reading workshop environment. We like to think about these behaviors on a continuum. This developmental continuum reflects a range of distinguishable behaviors common for

TABLE 8
Independent Reading Continuum of Self-Selection Behaviors

Reluctant	Transitional	Self-Directed
• Choose to read occasionally	• Eager to read and eager to please	• Choose to read all the time
• Need additional support beyond whole-group, small-group, and conferring to gain meaning from text	• Need basic support as found in whole-group, small-group, and conferring	• Need limited support—but may need nudging toward challenges
• Abandon a majority of the time—do not find a purpose in reading	• Finish most books—abandon due to difficulty, length, and interest	• Commit to finishing a book—abandon based on personal preferences
• Gain minimal meaning from text	• Read for surface information	• Understand at a deeper level
• Give minimal consideration to selecting just-right books	• Work toward matching self to just-right books	• Successfully select just-right books

elementary-age students (see Table 8). Seeing our readers on this continuum helps us set instructional objectives and learning goals, as well as meet individual needs. At one end of the Independent Reading Continuum is Reluctant and the characteristics that correspond to those self-selection behaviors. At the opposite end of the continuum is Self-Directed and the characteristics that correspond to those self-selection behaviors. Somewhere in the middle are Transitional behaviors. The students you will read about in this chapter each represent a different stage of development along this continuum (see Figure 28).

We use these self-selection behaviors as a guide for identifying when students are ready for more responsibility. When a majority of the students are exhibiting transitional behaviors, this may be a period of plateau according to the pattern of implementing BOOKMATCH (see Figure 1 in the Preface or other versions of this pattern in Chapters 2 through 4). This doesn't mean that you won't see some signs of all the self-selection behaviors in each Phase of Learning—in fact, students continue to challenge themselves with a variety of texts. Your students will move along the continuum as they build background knowledge, learn to self-select, and encounter a variety of texts.

Keep in mind that this is a developmental continuum. Because our goal is to meet each reader's developmental needs, the continuum merely

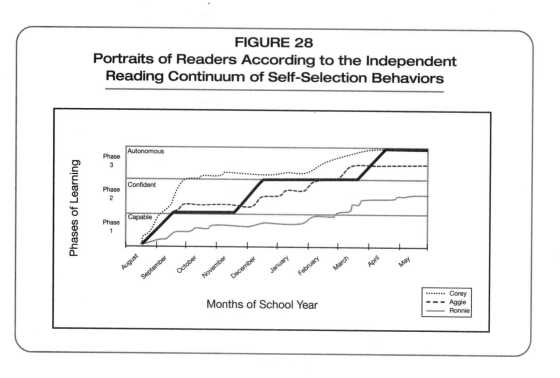

FIGURE 28
Portraits of Readers According to the Independent Reading Continuum of Self-Selection Behaviors

allows you to more effectively plan your implementation of BOOKMATCH to meet the specific needs of your readers. Whether a reader displayed reluctant, transitional, or self-directed behaviors, our instructional strategies were chosen in response to that individual's needs. When we implemented BOOKMATCH, we paid close attention to the effect of our instruction so that we could modify and differentiate as needed. Regardless of the behaviors, each of these three readers found success with self-selection and independent reading. Although our expectations are high, we meet each reader within his or her Zone of Proximal Development (ZPD; Vygotsky, 1978). We believe that you may connect to the three readers we present here and be reminded of similar readers from your own classroom. By reading about Ronnie, Aggie, and Corey, you will see the success that is possible.

The progress that all our readers made, not just Ronnie, Aggie, and Corey, was a result of the environment, instruction, and empowerment. Our preparation was purposeful, and so were the modeling, shared demonstrations, conferences, and assessments in which students participated. The goal was always self-selecting that just-right book. After all,

What more important decision does any reader make? If children learn how to choose a book they will enjoy or use competently, they are on the road to loving books and reading on their own. The right book at the right time is a gift of major proportions. (Skolnick, 2000, p. 129)

Ronnie: Reluctant Behavior

Ronnie began first grade with reluctant self-selection behaviors for independent reading (see Figure 29 for Ronnie's profile and self-portrait; his self-portrait hung throughout the year to show that he was a member of our class). He had a very rough kindergarten year. He had repeated instances of being sent home for language, violence toward others, and outbursts that typically led to yelling at teachers and administrators. Before the first-grade school year began, Ronnie was assessed using *An Observation Survey of Early Literacy Achievement* (Clay, 2006). Ronnie's scores on the assessments were as follows: Letter Identification, 53/54; Hearing and Recording Sounds in Words, 24/37; Writing Vocabulary, 23; Ohio Word Test, 19/20; Concepts About Print, 13/24; Instructional Text, Level 5. Ronnie's scores, in comparison to his peers, suggested that he had a partial

---

FIGURE 29
Profile and Self-Portrait for Ronnie

Reader Profile: Ronnie

Favorite Book: Any book from Magic Tree House series

Interests: Playing outside with friends; building blocks

Pets: 2 dogs, Baily and Bosco

Favorite Subject in School: Recess

Definition of Reading: I don't know

Something I'm really good at: Swimming

Someday I want to...be a teacher.

I love it when...I ride my bike.

Motivations: Choosing a treat from the treat jar, reading chapter books, playing basketball with older boys.

understanding of concepts about print and books in general as well as minimal writing vocabulary. While level 5 as an instructional level may not be that unusual for incoming first graders, in comparison to Ronnie's peers,

he was on the low end. Because of his limited background experiences with literacy, his scores on the early literacy assessments, and his previous behavioral concerns, he was referred to and qualified for Reading Recovery intervention in the first round (first semester). In the initial discussion with the classroom teacher and the support staff, the assumption was that Ronnie would need services the entire first-grade year.

One-on-one interviews with Ronnie showed that he wanted to learn and responded well to praise once he trusted the adult. He was well aware of what the others in the classroom were doing, and at times he would do his best to do the same. He had trouble making friends and did not take suggestions or criticism well.

Figure 30 illustrates Ronnie's progress in response to the implementation of BOOKMATCH. Throughout the year, he remained

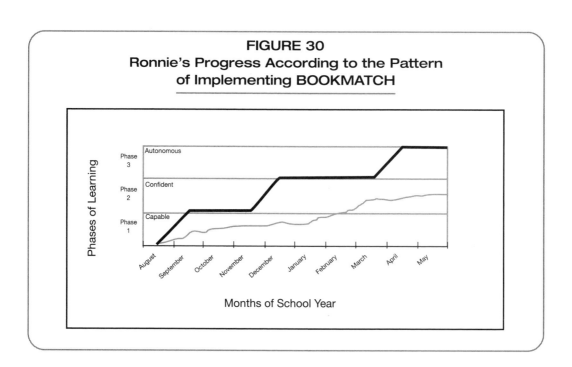

FIGURE 30
Ronnie's Progress According to the Pattern of Implementing BOOKMATCH

significantly below the typical pattern of learning. He remained in Phase 1: Capable for the majority of the school year, showing a distinct upward movement to Phase 2: Confident at the end of the year. His behaviors showed an increase in confidence with self-selection, but he didn't plateau at this phase, indicating he should continue practicing self-selection over the summer and in second grade in order to continue that upward movement of learning.

At the end of the first-grade school year, Ronnie was reassessed using *An Observation Survey of Early Literacy Achievement* (Clay, 2006). Ronnie's scores on this set of assessments were as follows: Letter Identification, 53/54; Hearing and Recording Sounds in Words, 37/37; Writing Vocabulary, 57; Ohio Word Test, 20/20; Concepts About Print, 17/24; Easy Text, Level 28. Ronnie's scores at this time, in comparison to his peers, suggested that he had a better understanding of concepts about print; however, he continued not to attend to details. He now had a stronger writing vocabulary, including hearing more sounds in words. Ronnie went from an instructional level of 5 to an easy level of 28. Although a word accuracy level of 28 (determined with running records) was well beyond the expectation of exiting first graders, Ronnie will still need additional support with comprehension. In our school, with post-assessment results, instructional levels of word accuracy reading are not always obtained. We do not push the reader into texts that may be developmentally inappropriate just to obtain a "hard" level. While the support staff originally believed that Ronnie would need a full year of Reading Recovery, his instruction was discontinued after the first round. Ronnie made remarkable progress as a result of the classroom experiences, the ideal practice environment, and the one-on-one instruction for reinforcement that we provided.

Instructional strategies for Ronnie were chosen to build on his strengths and reflect our understanding of reluctant behaviors. During Ronnie's first independent reading time, he selected *Mr. Popper's Penguins* (Atwater & Atwater, 1992), which was too difficult, too long, and too complex. However, Ronnie used his book stick correctly, sat at his table spot, did not disrupt anyone around him, opened the book, turned the pages, and sustained these behaviors throughout the reading time. For Ronnie, it was important to remember the purpose of the day. The purpose was getting students to understand the routines of reading workshop and specifically of independent reading. If we had questioned him about his practices, Ronnie may have become confused because he did what had just been modeled for him; however, we don't want to get ahead of ourselves or ahead of what Ronnie needs. These behaviors are important aspects of developing into a reader with which Ronnie needed opportunities to practice; he was simply not metacognitively ready to self-select successfully three weeks into the school year. Our instructional strategy was to allow him the needed practice in acquiring the reading behaviors appropriate for reading workshop. Students have to learn what it means to be a reader and identify what readers do. This is also called the Discourse (Gee, 1989) of readers and includes all the behaviors and talk that allow learners to gain access to this Discourse group. Ronnie reminded us that learning the Discourse of readers and eventually the Discourse of independent readers takes time.

Another instructional consideration for reluctant behaviors is to find something that connects to the readers' motivation and interests them. Ronnie called all books with pictures "baby books." While conferring with Ronnie, he asked, "Did Corey have to read those books first, too?" (He was referring to another student who was already reading chapter books). This conference was helpful because Ronnie revealed a motivation and desire to read a chapter book. Because our classroom library had a wide variety of books, we were able to suggest beginning chapter book series to Ronnie, such as Henry and Mudge by Cynthia Rylant, Nate the Great by Marjorie Weinman Sharmat, and Ricky Ricotta's Mighty Robot by Dav Pilkey. Nudging Ronnie into these books served the following purposes:

- Ronnie's reading endurance increased while building his vocabulary.

- He realized that he would not be restricted to "baby books."

- He believed that he could achieve like other chapter book readers during the independent reading time.

As with any reader who has challenged himself with more difficult texts, it is important to confer frequently to confirm that he is gaining meaning.

Finally, Ronnie's use of minimal criteria for self-selecting just-right books indicated a lack of understanding about books, their features, and the selection process. Therefore, while some students were becoming confident using the criteria already taught for BOOKMATCH, Ronnie needed more time to become confident with just the first few letters taught. Our instructional strategy here was to wait for Ronnie to exhibit confidence with *B* and *M* before expecting him to consider additional criteria.

Ronnie's reluctant behaviors are not uncommon in people who have limited literacy experiences. The most important instructional response to Ronnie was for us to accept where he was and to use his strengths to help him progress. Perhaps he didn't close the gap completely, but we're proud of the literacy foundation he acquired. We could have chosen to focus our attention elsewhere, but we believed that Ronnie was capable. He proved us right.

Aggie: Transitional Behavior

Aggie began first grade exhibiting transitional behaviors, with limited experiences in self-selection but eager to have control over her book choices (see Figure 31 for Aggie's profile and self-portrait). She had a typical kindergarten year; however, in comparison to her peers, her reading skills were low.

Before the first-grade school year began, Aggie was assessed using *An Observation Survey of Early Literacy Achievement* (Clay, 2006). Aggie's

---

FIGURE 31
Profile and Self-Portrait for Aggie

Reader Profile: Aggie

Favorite Book: *What Do You Do with a Tail Like This?* (Jenkins & Page, 2003)

Interests: Art, going to the park

Pets: Walter (dog)

Favorite Subject in School: Recess

Definition of Reading: You eat with your eyes.

Something I'm really good at: Swimming, I got two first place ribbons for backstroke.

Someday I want to...be a pop star.

I love it when...I walk my dog. I torture my brother.

Motivations: Reading in a comfy chair with a stuffed animal (reading buddy), getting out the watercolor paints, reading aloud to another classroom of students.

scores on the assessments were as follows: Letter Identification, 52/54; Hearing and Recording Sounds in Words, 33/37; Writing Vocabulary, 28; Ohio Word Test, 13/20; Concepts About Print, 17/24; Instructional Text, Level 5. Similar to Ronnie, Aggie's scores, in comparison to her peers, suggested that she had a basic understanding of concepts about print and books in general as well as limited sight word vocabulary. Like Ronnie, Aggie's word accuracy reading as determined on the running record was a level 5. While these scores may seem relatively low, she had made significant progress over the summer months. Even though Aggie did not qualify for the first round of Reading Recovery intervention, she was considered a priority for the second round (second semester).

Aggie is very witty and often lifted the spirits of other students by getting them to laugh. She would often ask if she didn't understand something. She was very aware of other readers' interests. She became intrigued with the choice option and the opportunity to spread out in comfy chairs during reading workshop.

Figure 32 illustrates Aggie's progress in response to the implementation of BOOKMATCH. Throughout the year, Aggie followed the typical pattern of implementing BOOKMATCH, the only difference being that she did not have a lengthy plateau in Phase 2: Confident. Once she began the upward movement in Phase 1, she continued that same slope of upward movement into Phase 3: Autonomous. When you consider the span of the school year, Aggie's results show a positive response to learning self-selection strategies and applying these strategies independently.

At the end of the first-grade school year, Aggie was reassessed using *An Observation Survey of Early Literacy Achievement* (Clay, 2006). Aggie's scores on this round of assessments were as follows: Letter Identification, 53/54; Hearing and Recording Sounds in Words, 37/37; Writing Vocabulary, 49; Ohio Word Test, 20/20; Concepts About Print, 23/24; Easy Text, Level 30. Aggie's scores suggested that she had a much better understanding of concepts about print. She recognized all sight words on the assessment. Most astonishing from these scores is Aggie's word accuracy level. She went from an instructional level of 5 to an easy level of 30. It was noted on her assessment that she also had strong comprehension and excellent fluency. While the support staff originally believed that Aggie would need Reading Recovery support, she exceeded expectations by second semester and was performing within the upper third of her peers.

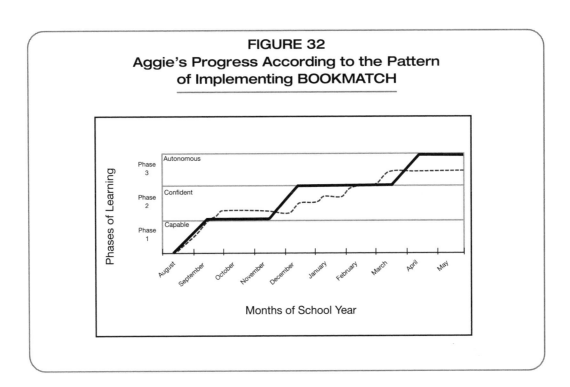

FIGURE 32
Aggie's Progress According to the Pattern of Implementing BOOKMATCH

Instructional strategies for Aggie needed to build on her strengths and reflect our understanding of transitional behaviors. Metacognitively, Aggie was ready within the first week to engage in self-selection experiences given basic instructional support through modeling, time to practice, guided groups, and conferences. Her eagerness to learn was refreshing and contagious.

Allowing Aggie choice during independent reading time proved to be the most effective instructional strategy for her transitional behaviors. Aggie encountered choice from the very first day of the school year when students had opportunities to just browse books that would eventually be sorted for the classroom library. Even decorating her book stick allowed for choice. Aggie took her first search for a just-right book very seriously. But the ultimate reward for Aggie was the opportunity to choose where she would read that just-right book. Aggie reacted very well to the "reward" of spreading out into a comfy chair. Later in the year we saw her escape into the world of Kevin Henkes's *Chrysanthemum* (2005). Because we recognized and supported choice as a motivator to read she practiced engaged reading, which we know was a critical factor for improving her reading ability.

Another way we supported Aggie with transitional behaviors was to allow her the time to really browse and think about her selections. She was meticulous about finding a just-right book, sometimes spending the whole independent reading time selecting a book. She was very familiar with the containers and would spend many minutes browsing, without disturbing others or losing track of what she needed to be doing. Her routine was to pull a container off the shelf, holding her book stick at the ready in case she wanted to pull anything out for further inspection. She looked at every book within one container to make sure nothing was missed. Then, she would put the container back on the shelf and place all of the selections in her book nook before going off to look in another container and repeat the process. We did not question Aggie's process within the routine and didn't panic that she was not sitting at her seat with just one book to read. It was important to allow Aggie to show her process because if we had stopped her, Aggie wouldn't have realized this was in fact productive (and efficient) behavior. The following day, Aggie would spend the independent reading time reading as many of those books selected as time would allow. She was often the last one cleaned up from independent reading because she didn't want to stop.

Aggie also benefited from the option to abandon. If she did so, we expected Aggie to talk through her reasons for abandoning using the language of BOOKMATCH. When Aggie said, "I've had these books too long so I decided I'm going to get rid of them," she was pulled for a conference as soon as possible to explain her decision. In the conference, Aggie revealed why the books did not fit her anymore. Sometimes, students lose interest, misjudge difficulty, or realize the length of the book is just too much work.

Teacher: Tell me why you want to abandon these books.

Aggie: Well, this one I read a bunch of times like almost 10 times, and this one I'm just not interested in anymore. And, well, this one was harder than I thought. I can't read all of it.

Teacher: I like that you were thinking about *H*—high-interest, because it's important to be interested in what you're reading, so you made a good decision to abandon when you weren't interested anymore. For this last book, you said it was harder than you thought. Do you mean that this book was not a good match for you because *M*—manageable text is actually too hard? The words are too hard? Can you show me what you mean? [Aggie read from one page of the book] You're right, you made a good decision to abandon this book, too.

We reinforced the terminology of BOOKMATCH by clarifying Aggie's responses and praising Aggie when she used the terminology independently. This reminded us that readers need conversations and conferences to discuss their reasons.

The combination of our instruction and the opportunity for choice created an ideal environment for Aggie to achieve beyond expectations. Aggie was able to close the achievement gap between herself and her most capable peers. Her success impressed us as she seemed to thrive on daily independent reading and her feelings of empowerment. Transitional behaviors need nurturing and consistent, successful literacy experiences. Instructional strategies for transitional behaviors might also be of benefit with reluctant behaviors or even self-directed behaviors. The key is to recognize an appropriate instructional response to the reading behaviors.

Corey: Self-Directed Behavior

Corey began first grade showing tendencies of self-directed behaviors (see Figure 33 for Corey's profile and self-portrait). He always chose to read, even during free choice times. Corey was shy, loved science and robots, and watched over his little sister. He liked to read the *Guinness Book of World Records* for pleasure. It was obvious that he visited the local library often. He even brought books from the library to read during independent reading time. His life experiences allowed him to understand harder content and vocabulary. Corey was already reading and rereading nonfiction books before he started first grade.

Corey was not screened with the whole battery of Reading Recovery assessments because he was already at an instructional level 16 and reading fluently. Even though we weren't worried about Corey, we still took time to take running records, check comprehension, and assess sight word vocabulary. Although Corey was already a good reader, we needed to make sure that his reading continued to progress. He was pulled for guided groups, received one-on-one conferences, and had weekly learning goals. He was assessed as often as all the other students throughout the school year.

FIGURE 33
Profile and Self-Portrait for Corey

Reader Profile: Corey

Favorite Book: Any book on planets

Interests: Cooking

Pets: Two fish, Leafy and Leafah

Favorite Subject in School: Writers' Workshop

Definition of Reading: You get to read books sometimes, so you can get to know more about things.

Something I'm really good at: Playing basketball.

Someday I want to...fly a plane.

I love it when...my mom gives me big hugs.

Motivations: Teach the class about what he just learned in his book, time at the take-apart center, work with Brock.

Figure 34 illustrates Corey's progress in response to the implementation of BOOKMATCH. For the first several months, Corey performed above the typical pattern of implementation. He had an initial, immediate upward slope, which is a good indication that the instruction was within his ZPD (Vygotsky, 1978). He moved quickly through Phase 1: Capable and Phase 2: Confident, but spent considerable time working through Phase 3: Autonomous. In Phase 3, he was able to perfect self-selection and build habits for lifelong literacy learning. Corey's results show a positive response to learning self-selection strategies and applying these strategies automatically.

At the end of the school year, exiting assessment using Rigby leveled texts (corresponding to Reading Recovery levels) showed that Corey could read accurately and comprehend at level 40. Comparatively, a reader with easy word accuracy at level 40 would be a secure third-grade reader. Corey was reading well beyond our first-grade expectations, and we imagine he will continue to perform at a high level.

Instructional strategies for Corey needed to build on his strengths and reflect our understanding of self-directed behaviors. Corey still had some learning to do. It didn't matter that he was reading at such a high level because we know that learning to read is ongoing. It's not just that you learn to read and then you're done. We wanted to make sure that he

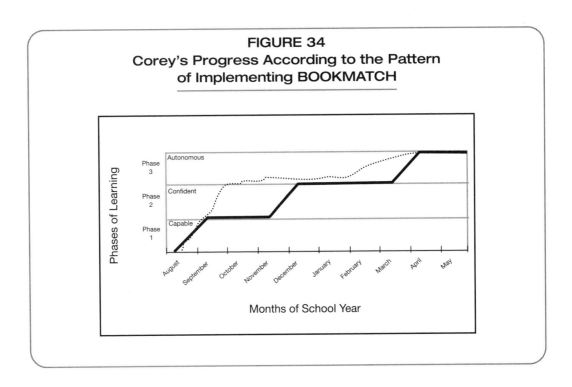

FIGURE 34
**Corey's Progress According to the Pattern
of Implementing BOOKMATCH**

was not ignored because he came in reading well. He, too, needed instructional attention.

Corey appeared confident when choosing books for independent reading. He found books quickly, sat and read them, appeared engaged, and returned books to the containers. He seemed to have a good grasp of the kinds of books that were just right for him. However, conferences revealed that he had been choosing "easy" books. Our first instructional strategy was to allow Corey to choose books in his comfort zone while he was still learning the workshop routines. Eventually, when we realized that he was not moving beyond easy books, we shared our running records as a way to explain that he needed to challenge himself during independent reading. We went so far as to explain what the check marks meant and that he had all check marks on every single book that he chose. While many students were using *M*—manageable text to make sure the text was not too difficult, Corey needed to think about *M* to make sure texts weren't too easy. Because Corey could decode most of the words in his selections, he needed to think about expanding his vocabulary. He waited for the teacher to tell him he was ready for chapter books even though he had been ready for awhile. He initially looked at the Magic Tree House series by Mary Pope Osborne, but the Stanley series by Jeff Brown became a more comfortable starting place for him to grow. Follow-up conferences were necessary to make sure that he continued to challenge himself. Because he caught on to things so quickly, he needed weekly monitoring.

Another instructional strategy used with self-directed behaviors is to expand knowledge of genres. Primary-age readers are more often exposed to fiction texts, but Corey typically selected nonfiction. His selections were based on his interests in science and robotics. A goal for Corey was to broaden his exposure to a wide variety of genres. We knew that this exposure would serve him well and balance his reading experiences. When Corey chose *Stanley in Space* (Brown, 2003), he was thinking about his interests, but also experiencing the treatment of a science topic within fiction. Corey found he was able to understand fictional texts at a deeper level because he brought significant background knowledge to his selection.

Eventually, Corey exhausted the nonfiction books within our first-grade classroom library. He completely mastered the reading workshop routine and never had to be redirected. To keep Corey engaged and challenged, our instructional strategy was to allow him access to more books. We made arrangements with other teachers in the building to allow Corey into their rooms, with book stick in hand, to select from their libraries. Corey looked for books in the other first-grade classroom, both second-grade classrooms, and in a third-grade classroom during the second half of the year. Corey took full advantage of this opportunity and rose to the level of responsibility with which we had empowered him. Allowing Corey access to more books and books with higher complexity was important for his growth as a reader. Of course, we continued to monitor his selections for *T*—topic appropriateness during conferences.

What would have happened to Corey if he had been limited to just our classroom library? He likely would have become bored, less engaged, and unproductive. We probably would have had to redirect him often. Instead, we supported his self-directed behaviors. Self-directed behaviors need attention too, but in a more targeted way because students who exhibit these behaviors are secure in their own abilities. In other words, they know what they can do, and such students can be taught in a more in-depth, sophisticated manner.

We know that Ronnie may still exhibit reluctant behaviors as he moves to the next grade, but we are confident that in a similar environment, he will continue to move along the continuum. Next year, when Ronnie's second-grade teacher says, "It's independent reading time," Ronnie will know exactly what to do. He'll be able to feel success right away. We know that Aggie's transitional behaviors remained until the end of the year, but we are confident that she will enter second grade as a self-directed reader. We know that Corey left first grade a very strong reader with self-directed behaviors. As a 7-year-old, Corey should challenge himself but consider the topic appropriateness of his selections. Based on what we saw in first grade, Corey will thrive when reading content texts in the upper grades.

Reflection Point

Who do the students in this chapter remind you of? How do you see BOOKMATCH supporting students like Ronnie, Aggie, and Corey in your classroom?

Reproducibles

BOOKMATCH Poster

B Book Length

O Ordinary Language

O Organization

K Knowledge Prior to Book

M Manageable Text

A Appeal to Genre

T Topic Appropriateness

C Connection

H High-Interest

Student Comment Form for Primary-Grade Readers

Criteria for Choosing Books	Student Comments
B **Book Length** Is this length too little, just right, or too much?	
O **Ordinary Language** Does it make sense and sound like talk?	
O **Organization** How is the book structured?	
K **Knowledge Prior to Book** What do I already know about this topic, this book, or this author?	
M **Manageable Text** Are the words too easy, just right, or too hard?	
A **Appeal to Genre** What is the genre and do I know this genre?	
T **Topic Appropriateness** Am I comfortable with the topic of this book?	
C **Connection** Can I relate and make a connection to another book or real life experience?	
H **High-Interest** Am I interested in finding out more?	

BOOKMATCH: How to Scaffold Student Book Selection for Independent Reading by Linda Wedwick and Jessica Ann Wutz.
© 2008 by the International Reading Association. May be copied for classroom use.

Student Comment Form for Intermediate-Grade Readers

Criteria for Choosing Books	Student Comments
B **Book Length** ✓ Is this a good length for me? ✓ Do I feel like committing to this book?	
O **Ordinary Language** ✓ Turn to any page and read aloud. ✓ Does the text sound natural? ✓ Does it flow? Does it make sense?	
O **Organization** ✓ How is the book structured? ✓ Are chapters short or long?	
K **Knowledge Prior to Book** ✓ Read the title, view the cover page, or read the summary on the back of the book. ✓ What do I already know about this topic, this book, or this author?	
M **Manageable Text** ✓ Begin reading the book. ✓ Will this book provide the right amount of challenge? ✓ Do I understand what I read?	
A **Appeal to Genre** ✓ What is the genre? ✓ Have I read this genre before? ✓ What can I expect from this genre?	
T **Topic Appropriateness** ✓ Am I comfortable with the topic of this book? ✓ Do I feel like I am ready to read about this topic?	
C **Connection** ✓ Can I relate to this book? ✓ Can I make a connection?	
H **High-Interest** ✓ Am I interested in this book? ✓ Do others recommend this book? ✓ What is my purpose for reading this book?	

Independent Reading Attitude Survey

You read each statement silently as I read them aloud. After each statement, circle the word that best describes your reading behaviors.

1. I enjoy free reading time at school.	Always	Sometimes	Never
2. I feel that books are boring.	Always	Sometimes	Never
3. I like to recommend good books to my friends.	Always	Sometimes	Never
4. I read if the teacher assigns it as homework.	Always	Sometimes	Never
5. I think reading is hard.	Always	Sometimes	Never
6. I like to read when I have spare time.	Always	Sometimes	Never
7. If I start reading a book, I finish the book.	Always	Sometimes	Never
8. It takes me a long time to read a book.	Always	Sometimes	Never
9. I like to read when I'm not at school.	Always	Sometimes	Never
10. I try to find books by my favorite authors.	Always	Sometimes	Never
11. I'd rather watch TV than read a book.	Always	Sometimes	Never
12. I only like certain types of books.	Always	Sometimes	Never
13. I think I am a good reader.	Always	Sometimes	Never
14. I learn new things from free reading.	Always	Sometimes	Never

Please respond to the following in writing.

1. What do you think is the easiest thing about reading when you are alone?

2. What do you think is the hardest thing about reading when you are alone?

3. What do you like about reading alone?

4. What do you dislike about reading alone?

5. Describe your favorite place to read and why you like to read there.

6. Who do you know who likes to read?_____

7. How do you know this person likes to read?

8. Who do you know who doesn't like to read? _____

9. How do you know this person doesn't like to read?

10. Are you more like the person who likes to read or the person who doesn't like to read? Why do you think so?

Originally published in Wutz, J.A., & Wedwick, L. (2005). BOOKMATCH: Scaffolding book selection for independent reading. *The Reading Teacher, 59*(1), 16–32.
BOOKMATCH: How to Scaffold Student Book Selection for Independent Reading by Linda Wedwick and Jessica Ann Wutz. © 2008 by the International Reading Association. May be copied for classroom use.

Selection Criteria Survey

Do I think about how long the book is?	☐ Always ☐ Sometimes ☐ Never ☐ I don't know
Do I think about the style of writing? Does it sound like talk?	☐ Always ☐ Sometimes ☐ Never ☐ I don't know
Do I think about how the book is organized?	☐ Always ☐ Sometimes ☐ Never ☐ I don't know
Do I think about how much I already know about the topic of the book?	☐ Always ☐ Sometimes ☐ Never ☐ I don't know
Do I think about how hard the words are?	☐ Always ☐ Sometimes ☐ Never ☐ I don't know
Do I think about the genre, or what type of book it is?	☐ Always ☐ Sometimes ☐ Never ☐ I don't know
Do I think about how comfortable I am with the topic of the book?	☐ Always ☐ Sometimes ☐ Never ☐ I don't know
Do I think about how I can relate to the book?	☐ Always ☐ Sometimes ☐ Never ☐ I don't know
Do I think about how interested I am in the topic, author, or illustrator?	☐ Always ☐ Sometimes ☐ Never ☐ I don't know
How often do I finish a book I select?	Always 5 Usually 4 Sometimes 3 Rarely 2 Never 1
What are some reasons why I might not finish a book I start reading?	

My Reading Log

Title: _____

Author: _____

Am I at the end of this book?   YES   NO

Will I come back to this book?   YES   NO

Response:

_____

_____

_____

Running Record and Conference   Date:

My Independent Reading Log

What did I read?	Today's date is...	My response

Independent Reader BOOKMATCH Rubric

Name: _____ Date: _____

	Consistent Evidence (2)	Some Evidence (1)	No Evidence (0)
Uses previously taught criteria to make book selections.			
Successfully chooses just-right books.			
Monitors engagement with book selection.			

Total Points _____

Reading Workshop Rubric

Name: _____ Date: _____

	Independent (3)	Needs Some Support (2)	Limited Independence (1)	No Evidence (0)
Reads independently for extended periods.				
Comprehends texts.				
Chooses just-right books.				
Participates in conferences and guided groups.				
Uses reading strategies.				
Records information on logs or student comment forms.				
Respects reading environment (uses book nook and book stick, moves about quietly, does not disturb other readers).				

Total Points _____

REFERENCES

Allington, R. (2005/2006, December/January). What counts as evidence in evidence-based education? *Reading Today, 23*, 16.

Anderson, R.C., Hiebert, E.H., Scott, J.A., & Wilkinson, I.A.G. (1985). *Becoming a nation of readers: The report of the Commission on Reading.* Washington, DC: National Institute of Education.

Anderson, R.C., & Pearson, P.D. (1984). A schema-theoretic view of basic processes in reading comprehension. In P.D. Pearson, R. Barr, M.L. Kamil, & P.B. Mosenthal (Eds.), *Handbook of reading research* (pp. 255–291). New York: Longman.

Andrade, H.G. (2005). Teaching with rubrics: The good, the bad, and the ugly. *College Teaching, 53*(1), 27–30.

Atwell, N. (1998). *In the middle: New understandings about writing, reading, and learning.* Portsmouth, NH: Heinemann.

Bintz, W.P. (1993). Resistant readers in secondary education: Some insights and implications. *Journal of Reading, 36*(8), 604–615.

Calkins, L. (2001). *The art of teaching reading.* New York: Longman.

Cambourne, B. (1988). *The whole story: Natural learning and the acquisition of literacy in the classroom.* New York: Scholastic.

Chandler-Olcott, K. (2002). Scaffolding love: A framework for choosing books for, with, and by adolescents. *Illinois Reading Council Journal, 30*(2), 10–23.

Clay, M. (2006). *An observation survey of early literacy achievement* (2nd ed.). Portsmouth, NH: Heinemann.

Crain, W. (2000). *Theories of development: Concepts and applications* (4th ed.). Upper Saddle River, NJ: Prentice Hall.

D'Arcy, J. (1989). Talking in the reading conference. In J. Dwyer (Ed.), *A sea of talk* (pp. 21–31). Portsmouth, NH: Heinemann.

Davis, M. (2005, January). Building classroom libraries with shelf life. *School Talk, 10*(2), 4.

Fountas, I.C., & Pinnell, G.S. (1996). *Guided reading: Good first teaching for all children.* Portsmouth, NH: Heinemann.

Gambrell, L.B., Palmer, B.M., Codling, R.M., & Mazzoni, S.A. (1996). Assessing reading motivation. *The Reading Teacher, 49*(7), 518–533.

Gardiner, S. (2005). *Building student literacy through sustained silent reading.* Alexandria, VA: Association for Supervision and Curriculum Development.

Gee, J. (1989). Literacy, discourse, and linguistics: Introduction. *Journal of Education, 171*(1), 5–17.

Goodman, Y.M. (1985). Kidwatching: Observing children in the classroom. In A. Jaggar & M.T. Smith-Burke (Eds.), *Observing the language learner* (pp. 9–18). Newark, DE: International Reading Association.

Goodman, Y.M. (1996). Revaluing readers while readers revalue themselves: Retrospective miscue analysis. *The Reading Teacher, 49*(8), 600–609.

Grosvenor, L. (2004). *Differentiated instruction from a librarian's perspective.* Retrieved February 8, 2008, from www.newhorizons.org/strategies/differentiated/grosvenor.htm

Hindley, J. (1996). *In the company of children.* York, ME: Stenhouse.

Ivey, G. (1999). A multicase study in the middle school: Complexities among young adolescent readers. *Reading Research Quarterly, 34*(2), 172–192.

Ivey, G., & Broaddus, K. (2000). Tailoring the fit: Reading instruction and middle school readers. *The Reading Teacher, 54*(1), 68–78.

Johns, J.L., & Lenski, S.D. (2001). *Improving reading: Strategies and resources* (3rd ed.). Dubuque, IA: Kendall/Hunt.

Jones, J.A. (2006). Student-involved classroom libraries. *The Reading Teacher, 59*(6), 576–580.

Keeping kids reading: New study shows drop after age 8, but parents can help. (2006, August/September). *Reading Today, 24*, 3.

Krashen, S. (2001). More smoke and mirrors: A critique of the National Reading Panel Report on Fluency. *Phi Delta Kappan, 83*(2), 119–123.

Lanier, E., & Lenski, S.D. (2008). *Developing an independent reading program: Grades 4–12*. Norwood, MA: Christopher-Gordon Publishers.

Lenski, S.D., & Nierstheimer, S.L. (2004). *Becoming a teacher of reading: A developmental approach*. Upper Saddle River, NJ: Prentice Hall.

McKenna, M.C., & Kear, D.J. (1990). Measuring attitude toward reading: A new tool for teachers. *The Reading Teacher, 43*(9), 626–639.

Morrow, L.M., Pressley, M., Smith, J.K., & Smith, M. (1997). The effect of a literature-based program integrated into literacy and science instruction with children from diverse backgrounds. *Reading Research Quarterly, 32*(1), 54–76.

National Institute of Child Health and Human Development. (2000). *Report of the National Reading Panel. Teaching children to read: An evidence-based assessment of the scientific research literature on reading and its implications for reading instruction* (NIH Publication No. 00-4769). Washington, DC: U.S. Government Printing Office.

Pearson, P.D. (1982). A primer for schema theory. *Volta Review, 84*(1), 25–34.

Pearson, P.D., & Gallagher, M.C. (1983). The instruction of reading comprehension. *Contemporary Educational Psychology, 8*(3), 317–344.

Piaget, J. (1973). *The child and reality: Problems of genetic psychology* (A. Rosin, Trans.). New York: Grossman Publishers.

Pierce, K.M. (1999). "I am a level 3 reader": Children's perceptions of themselves as readers. *The New Advocate, 12*(4), 359–375.

Pilgreen, J.L. (2000). *The SSR handbook: How to organize and manage a sustained silent reading program*. Portsmouth, NH: Heinemann.

Robb, L. (2004). Responsive teaching: Meeting every student's needs. *School Talk, 9*(3), 5–6.

Rog, L.J., & Burton, W. (2001/2002). Matching texts and readers: Leveling early reading materials for assessment and instruction. *The Reading Teacher, 55*(4), 348–356.

Rosenblatt, L. (1991). Literature—S.O.S.! *Language Arts, 68*(6), 444–448.

Routman, R. (2003). *Reading essentials: The specifics you need to teach reading well*. Portsmouth, NH: Heinemann.

Skolnick, D. (2000). *More than meets the eye*. Portsmouth, NH: Heinemann.

Stanford, P., & Siders, J.A. (2001). Authentic assessment for intervention. *Intervention in School & Clinic, 36*(3), 163–167.

Stanovich, K.E. (1986). Matthew effects in reading: Some consequences of individual differences in the acquisition of literacy. *Reading Research Quarterly, 21*(4), 360–407.

Szymusiak, K., & Sibberson, F. (2001). *Beyond leveled books: Supporting transitional readers in grades 2–5*. Portland, ME: Stenhouse.

Tomlinson, C. (1999). *The differentiated classroom: Responding to the needs of all learners*. Alexandria, VA: Association for Supervision and Curriculum Development.

Tullock-Rhody, R., & Alexander, J.E. (1980). A scale for assessing attitudes toward reading in secondary schools. *Journal of Reading, 23*(7), 609–614.

Vygotsky, L.S. (1978). *Mind in society: The development of higher psychological processes* (M. Cole, V. John-Steiner, S. Scribner, & E. Souberman, Eds. & Trans.). Cambridge, MA: Harvard University Press.

Wedwick, L., & Wutz, J.A. (2006). Thinking outside the bookbox: Using BOOKMATCH to develop independent book selection. *Voices From the Middle, 14*(1), 20–29.

Willis, S., & Mann, L. (2000, Winter). Differentiating instruction: Finding manageable ways to meet individual needs. *Curriculum Update*. Retrieved March 13, 2007, from www.ascd.org/ed_topics/cu2000win_willis.html

Wolfe, P. (2001). *Brain matters: Translating research into classroom practice*. Alexandria, VA: Association for Supervision and Curriculum Development.

Woolfolk, A. (2000). *Educational psychology* (8th ed.). Boston: Allyn & Bacon.

Wutz, J.A., & Wedwick, L. (2005). BOOKMATCH: Scaffolding book selection for independent reading. *The Reading Teacher, 59*(1), 16–32.

Yoon, J.-C. (2002). Three decades of sustained silent reading: A meta-analytic review of the effects of SSR on attitude toward reading. *Reading Improvement, 39*(4), 186–195.

Children's Literature Cited

Atwater, R., & Atwater, F. (1992). *Mr. Popper's penguins*. Boston: Little, Brown.

Brown, J. (2003). *Stanley in space*. New York: HarperCollins.

Brown, M. (1976). *Arthur's nose*. Boston: Little, Brown.

Brown, M. (2005). *Arthur's tooth*. Boston: Little, Brown.

Cowley, J. (1997). *Talk, talk, talk*. Crystal Lake, IL: Rigby.

Gunzi, C. (2001). *The best book of big cats*. Boston: Kingfisher.

Henkes, K. (1996). *Chrysanthemum*. New York: Mulberry Books.

Jenkins, S., & Page, R. (2003). *What do you do with a tail like this?* Boston: Houghton Mifflin.

Pinkwater, D.M. (1993). *The big orange splot*. New York: Scholastic.

Schmidt, D. (2005). *Racing stripes*. New York: Scholastic.

INDEX

Note. Page numbers followed by the letters *f*, *t*, and *r* indicate figures, tables, and reproducibles, respectively.